Beauty in Barren Places
Seeing God's Goodness Here and Now

Betsy Herman

Cover Design: Rebekah Hauck, Peachtree Graphic Designs

Author Photo: Mike Herman

To my husband Mike,
thank you for loving me and
always pointing me toward
the goodness of God.

Though the fig tree does not bud and there are no grapes on the vines,
though the olive crop fails and the fields produce no food,
though there are no sheep in the pen and no cattle in the stalls,
yet I will rejoice in the LORD, I will be joyful in God my Savior.
Habakkuk 3:17-18

I would have lost heart, unless I had believed
that I would see the goodness of the Lord in the land of the living.
Psalm 27:13 (NKJV)

CONTENTS

FOREWORD

By Natasha Metzler

When I was twelve years old, my family moved from Alaska to Florida. Yes, that's basically the most drastic move you can make while still staying in the United States. And to be honest? I wasn't too happy about it.

There were the typical preteen reasons for my dislike, such as leaving my friends behind and going to a new school and church right when I was trying to figure out who I was anyway. But I also had some other reasons for disliking Florida. It was hot and brown and flat and sandy. Sure, there were beaches, but where we lived in Alaska had beaches too. And unlike Florida, Alaska had richness and brilliant scenery and wildlife. The Florida we moved to was the suburbs where there were houses and sidewalks. It felt empty to me. Like a sandy, barren desert.

The first year after our move was rough. Any excitement from a new house and new things quickly faded, and all I had left was a bitterness that was quickly taking over my close relationships. I was bitter about the heat that kept me trapped indoors, bitter about the blandness of our surroundings, and bitter that my friends weren't with me. I smiled at church but came home and was grumpy with my family—because my true heart was full of ugliness over our circumstances.

Finally, one afternoon my mom confronted me, and I yelled out my frustrations into our white tiled kitchen. "I just want to go home to Alaska," I insisted. It wasn't fair that they forced us all to move to Florida. It wasn't fair that I now had to contend with getting heat exhaustion because my body wasn't adjusting to the high temperatures very well. It wasn't fair that my brothers made friends easily because they were outgoing and good looking, while I struggled to form deep relationships because of being introverted.

All my bitterness poured out in an ugly torrent of words that left my mother standing across from me with her eyebrows slightly raised. Once I finished, she quietly stared at me for a moment before speaking. "You know, Tasha," she began, "whether you like it here or not isn't really the point. This is where God has you." And then she asked me the real question—was I going to surrender to the God who placed me somewhere I didn't want to be? Or was I going to allow bitterness to rule my heart and mind forever?

That afternoon brought a drastic change to my teenage years, because somehow the reality of her words broke through the curtain of my self-absorbed and bitter thought patterns. It clicked in my head that being angry wasn't going to change my circumstances, but maybe, somehow, trusting and surrendering could bring about good from what I thought was only ugly.

There is something glorious that happens when we surrender. Our sight, which can be dimmed and marred by bitterness and selfishness and anger, begins to clear. Things we never noticed before materialize in the distance and a deeper truth about where we are becomes part of our everyday lives.

Florida, it turned out, is beautiful. Still barren in some places, as one would expect any giant sandbar to be, but it carries its own breathtaking pieces of loveliness.

In Florida you can see for miles across rolling flat land. When thunderstorms roll through, the sky will pile high with clouds of blue and gray and green. Below what first appears to be just brown barrenness around the edges of the sidewalks and houses you can find flora that blooms during the right seasons into such brightly colored blossoms, you almost feel like they couldn't possibly be real.

Florida is beautiful in its own right. Different than Alaska, of course, but still coated with beauty if you're bothering to look for it. And as my heart began to look around with openness and new sight, I found all the things I needed for survival—including life-long friendships and a relationship with the Father that would transform my heart and mind.

When Betsy asked me to write a foreword for her new book and mentioned that the name was *Beauty in Barren Places*, all I could picture was riding a bike down the sidewalk in Florida and realizing in shock that even though it still wasn't my favorite place—it really was beautiful there.

Learning that truth about what appeared to me as a physically barren place was vital in my walk with the Lord because years later I would step into an emotional and spiritually barren place that would leave my soul cracked and empty. Infertility, or as the Bible calls it, barrenness, would mark over a decade of my life with a harshness that left me raw and vulnerable and struggling with bitterness in a deeper and darker way than I'd ever experienced before.

The question my mother asked me years before became a fight of epic proportions in my heart: was I going to surrender to the God who placed me somewhere I didn't want to be?

This question is just the beginning of a wild adventure—because once we accept the harshness of surrender, we're welcomed into the beauty that can be found in the most barren of places.

As you read this book you'll be encouraged by stories and wisdom that will center your heart on this deep abiding truth: *there is beauty in barren places.*

So come along on this journey through stories about sickness and loss, monkeys and tarantulas, marriage and singleness, infertility and birth—but more specifically, God being the ultimate source of all beauty and being untethered by time and circumstances.

He will meet us in the barren places and paint them with beauty—teaching us to taste joy no matter what our surroundings are like. And I pray this book will encourage your heart to surrender to Him in a new and life-changing way.

Natasha Metzler

author of *Pain Redeemed: When Our Deepest Sorrows Meet God*

CHAPTER 1

STRANDED

God is faithful.

1 Corinthians 1:9

"You need to sit up, we're about to land," the airplane pilot said, glancing at me over his shoulder. Weak from the mysterious illness plaguing my body, the sound of the small airplane had quickly lulled me to sleep. The pilot and his buddy sat in the two front seats, and I was the only passenger in the back. After spending most of the flight lying across the seat, I slowly sat up. I looked out my window, gazing at the Kenyan countryside. The world below me looked sunny and green that May.

As the plane descended, my eyes searched for a dirt landing strip among grassy fields and trees. Before I knew it, we landed in a field. *That must have been the landing strip*, I thought.

I stepped off the plane to be greeted by a missionary I had met several times in my childhood, a family friend who visited us over the years. I climbed into a Land Rover with the missionary doctor and his young child, and he drove down the rutted dirt roads toward their family home.

For many years, my father, a family physician, has pursued his calling by traveling to South Sudan nearly every spring and fall. When the political unrest there hinders him from going, he goes to another needy part of the world. For many years, he regularly traveled to an area near the Lopit mountains of South Sudan. Caring for these people is one of my dad's greatest passions in life. He works hard to prepare, travel, and live in Africa for weeks at a time, where he tends to many different medical needs including malnourishment, neck pain from carrying heavy loads on the head and shoulders, spear wounds, and animal bites.

One spring when I was in college I made plans to join him on a trip to Sudan. (This was before the country split in two.) From what I had heard of events in Sudan, I imagined that Sudan at the turn of the century resembled images such as what I saw described in Lamentations 2:12 "...their lives ebb away in their mothers' arms." The country was torn by war, the land stripped bare, and many people were desperate. My mind and heart were ready to reach out to people in need, to serve in any way that I could on this medical outreach.

I prepared for my trip to Sudan: first requesting time off from my part-time job at a daycare, then raising the necessary financial support. With the blessing of my church and family, I headed to the airport with my dad and several others.

We flew from North Carolina to London, where we spent our 12-hour layover sightseeing. Because of jet lag, my mind felt as foggy as

London looked, yet despite my grogginess I still felt a sense of awe when I looked at Big Ben, watched the changing of the guard, and listened to people discuss the Rosetta Stone in various languages inside the British Museum. After seeing as much as we could in one sleep-deprived day, we boarded our flight from London to Nairobi, Kenya.

Having gone through some vegetarian phases in my teen years, I ate a vegetarian meal on the plane that night. I don't remember what it was, but I do remember that I ate something different from the rest of our team. I felt a little queasy during our travels, but between flying, jet lag, hours of walking in London, and the excitement of going to Africa, I didn't think much of it. We rested at a guest house in the capital of Kenya before taking a small plane to the Kenya-Sudan border, where we stayed for one night before flying to our destination.

That evening my stomach began hurting and I had a feeling that sickness was coming. I spent that entire night visiting the toilet (which was more like a squatty potty or a hole in the ground) or lying in my bed vomiting into the plastic bags that we pulled out of our luggage. I cannot recall a stomach sickness that has ever hit me harder. Despite the medications offered by my personal physician (a.k.a. Dad), I was very ill. My father had to make a tough decision that night, and he ultimately chose to send me back into Kenya to stay with family friends while he and the team continued forward with their mission trip. He felt it would be unwise to fly me into a remote area that lacked medical care I could potentially need if the sickness continued. At that moment, I was too sick to care.

The team headed north to Sudan, and I flew south in the care of a missionary pilot. I slept through that plane ride, until the pilot warned me that we were about to land.

I bounced back from the stomach illness in the next few days, and my tears flowed as I felt homesick for family. I longed for something familiar. I was stranded in a foreign country, where the air was cooler than I had expected. I bundled up in my light jacket for a week, read book after book in the family's library, and interacted with the people around me. Also staying with this family were some young medical students. One night they invited me to watch a movie with them— some story set in Africa that involved people camping in tents in an area where lions roamed and occasionally attacked. Knowing that my dad and his team were sleeping in tents in an area where lions could be roaming made me too nervous, so I didn't join in for movie night.

My initial journey to Africa was difficult. It was not what I had planned or expected. I felt extremely disappointed to be so close to my destination yet so far away. What caused my sickness in Africa? I don't know. Maybe it was food poisoning, maybe it was spiritual warfare. I may never know, but I do know that sickness led to disappointment that week.

Brokenhearted, I spoke to my mom by phone, generating a hefty phone bill in that era before internet phone calls were available. I sobbed as I told her I just wanted to be able to go on to Sudan. But I couldn't. I was stuck in a small town in Kenya while my father and his team were miles away in the bush of Sudan, and the rest of my family and friends were back home in the United States.

However, God reminded me of something during that trip. As I spent time seeing various aspects of life in Kenya, visiting a children's hospital, and sharing a meal in the tiny apartment of a local woman, God reminded me that just a few years earlier I had been fascinated by Kenya. In high school, I had sponsored a child there through a charitable organization. Each month I donated my hard earned babysitting money to sponsor a teen girl close to my own age, helping her to attend school and receive the food and clothing she needed. My sponsorship had sparked an interest in that country, and as a school assignment, I wrote a paper about Kenya, dreaming about someday visiting there. In the few years between high school and my first visit to Africa, I had forgotten that dream.

But God had not forgotten.

Someday had become today. I hadn't planned to spend a week in Kenya; instead I had intended to spend that time in Sudan with my Dad and his team. I realized in that moment, however, that God was answering my prayers by birthing a dream that had been pushed aside in my heart. I had forgotten my desire to visit Kenya, but He had not.

God took me to Kenya while closing my door to Sudan. He showed me the vast beauty of the great Rift Valley. He gave me a small taste of Kenyan food and culture as I sat in a tiny one-room apartment with another American and a local woman. God allowed me to rest and recover in a safe place, and He demonstrated His goodness by reminding me that He answers our prayers, even when they're no longer on our minds.

At the end of the week, I reunited with my Dad and his teammates, and we flew back across the Atlantic ocean to resume our normal lives, but I was forever changed by that experience. Since then, God has continually shown me that He is writing the story of my life differently than I might choose to write it, and His plan and intentions are always good.

CHAPTER 2

SEASHORE

**He is the Maker of heaven and earth,
the sea, and everything in them—He remains faithful forever.**

Psalm 146:6

So much of life is like the ebb and the flow of the ocean, the coming and going, the fullness and emptiness. The flow—when the ocean comes rushing in, and everything seems abundant, even to the point of feeling overwhelming. The ebb—when excitement fades, life feels dull. Relationships ebb and flow. Finances ebb and flow. So do moods and energy and hope.

Throughout our first decade as a couple, my husband and I enjoyed strolling along the sandy shores of the Atlantic Ocean near his childhood home. We've moved around, so depending on where we are living at the time, we try to visit his family in his hometown several times a year.

Over the years, we have loved walking together along that particular beach. I remember specific walks there, reconnecting with each other after a busy workweek. Hand-in-hand, we'd stroll along the seashore, discussing situations and people that matter to us. We discussed friendships, finances, and our future. We made memories there. On one of our beach outings, we learned that our preferred parking lot, which is part of a state park, takes their closing time seriously. Early in our dating relationship, we managed to stay at the beach past sunset and found ourselves locked inside the gate! We had to call the park ranger to unlock the gate so that we could return home.

We have spent time along the shore hunting for seashells, strolling into the sunset, and taking countless photos of the shells, the sand dunes and the golden sun setting beyond the pier. Each time we set foot on this beach, we stumbled upon beauty, never knowing what to expect.

As the two of us have walked with God as a couple for more than a decade, we've learned that He is a disrupter of our plans. Whether or not it makes sense, if we pause to ponder the story God is writing, we see that it's good. And even if it doesn't look good, we take a step of faith to believe that He is good. Once upon a time, we planned to get married and start a family a couple of years later. Instead my womb remained closed for seven years.

That beach has been a special place to immerse ourselves in focused conversation. Well, to be honest, we enjoyed such conversation for many years. Finally, a miracle happened, and we became pregnant, and learning to parent together became our new challenge. On our most recent visit to this particular seashore, we found ourselves focusing on our active toddler instead of immersing in conversation. We captured photos as she discovered the joy of splashing in the surf and digging in the sand.

We are in this new season of life—parenting together. Throughout the years we have walked up and down that beach in the heat and humidity of a Carolina summer, and we've explored the deserted beach in the dead of winter. Beauty is there, in the ebb and the flow.

Beauty and Barrenness

As I began writing this book, I contemplated the stories God has authored in my life. I grappled with disappointing situations, unmet longings, and life not going like I thought it should. It was as if God were whispering to me, "Look for My beauty in the barren places."

If you stand on the ocean's shore, looking out at the vast sea, you see something much bigger than yourself. You often see beauty, but sometimes you see storms. At times the sandy beach is covered with unique seashells, other days it's bare. Sometimes you see abundant life, other times you quickly sidestep to avoid setting your foot on a dead sea creature that washed ashore.

I'm learning that even in the empty spaces, God is still the Creator of beauty. His beauty can be found in barren places. He demonstrates His goodness always. I find it easy to see beauty in barrenness throughout nature: evidence of a winter ice storm glistening on leafless trees or a flower determined to bloom after struggling to grow through a crack in the sidewalk. One day someone handed me a postcard photo of Joshua Tree National Park. I've never visited that park, and the image that I held in my hand made me feel awe at the sight of the bristly, spiky trees that look like they were designed by Dr. Seuss. The Designer of all creativity planted them there, in the desert landscape, because He loves making barren places beautiful. He created something whimsical in a desert place that we might otherwise assume to be dry and lifeless. When our lives feel barren for any reason, such as prolonged singleness, infertility, financial struggles, relational emptiness—no matter why we feel barren, there is beauty to be found.

Definitions of barren include not reproducing or simply not yet pregnant. The term can refer to something that is desolate, lifeless, joyless. Wombs, bank accounts, and emotions can all seem barren. These barren places are simply empty spaces yearning to be filled with God's goodness.

Beauty was a word I didn't want to include in the title, because over the years I've felt more barren than beautiful. God created beauty. He has placed it everywhere. If your life feels more like a mess than a work of art, then let this book remind you that God makes messes into something beautiful. When we step back and see the story that God is writing with our lives, when we intentionally look for His good, we'll see beauty.

From God's perspective, He's crafting a beautiful tapestry. Often we're looking at the wrong side of the tapestry, focusing on what appears to be a tangled web of thread. It is just the back side of a work of art. When we look from God's perspective, we see a beautiful picture designed by our Creator's hand.

My life so far is not the story I would have written, tied neatly with a bow like a predictable happy Hallmark movie. However, as I contemplate all that God has done, I see the goodness of God. The barren seasons that we all experience are an opportunity to open our eyes to God's goodness. Acknowledging God's goodness and having an attitude of thankfulness toward Him is a key to living fully.

Psalm 27:13 says, "I remain confident of this: I will see the goodness of the Lord in the land of the living." Right here, right now, I can choose to look for God's goodness. I am determined to see God's goodness this year of my life. I can find His goodness today.

Although barrenness is a word I despised, it described seven years of my life in a physical sense. When I was thirty years old, my husband and I began trying to start our family, and we realized that it was not happening as quickly as we expected. Nearly five years later, I published my story in a book called *When Infertility Books Are Not Enough: Embracing Hope During Infertility*. I wrote a hope-filled book in the middle of that trial because God had given us hope that one day He would break through, even when we faced disappointment and grief month after month. The years following that publication were not easy emotionally, as our attempts of growing our family seemed futile, and our finances were tight. Life felt barren, so I poured myself into writing this book.

I finished the first draft of this manuscript early one summer. The next month, I took a pregnancy test, expecting it to be negative since that's all I'd ever known. I was surprised to discover that my womb finally carried new life! I suppose it was a glimmer of hope that caused me to take a test many months, just in case God had answered our prayers. I expected to see something negative that day, yet the little digital screen revealed one word that changed our lives with a "YES."

In that moment, God said yes to years of prayer over my womb. In that moment, I was no longer physically barren. What I discovered in the months of pregnancy that followed was abounding joy, because in an instant God lifted the sorrow and grief that had clouded my heart during years of infertility. Our tiny baby brought us so much joy while she grew within me. (She continually brings us joy every day now that she's an active little toddler.) My husband and I paved the way for joy and peace throughout our pregnancy, because in our season of physical barrenness, we consistently reminded ourselves that God was and is good toward us. In our disappointment, we reminded ourselves of God's faithfulness. During that time period, I often wore a t-shirt that said "Choose Joy," so that when I looked in the mirror on the hard days, I would remember to find the good, to discover joy in my sorrow.

I have learned that barrenness is more than infertility. Any area of a person's life can feel lifeless.

Maybe the struggle to have a baby isn't your story. Maybe a relationship that once felt life-giving is now feeling dried up. Maybe you're getting older, or family life and career paths have shifted, and you're struggling to find the abundant life that you once knew. It could be that you're struggling to know any feelings of joy or contentment. Your life just feels difficult, or your emotions are drained. You're not alone in these barren feelings.

After several years of working on this book, it seems that the right time to publish it is in the wake of the COVID-19 pandemic. I didn't plan it this way; it's simply the year I have enough time to focus on it amidst many major changes within our family. The year 2020 brought so much shaking, disruption, and change into the lives of everyone I know. A painful year, a difficult year, a depressing year would be how many describe it. Yet within the dark and empty places, if we look for it, we will see the light of our Heavenly Father. His goodness always shines into darkness.

Embracing the Story

My story of being stranded in Kenya is one I hadn't considered in quite some time until I began writing this book. Many things have happened since my first trip to Africa. Looking back over my adult life so far, there has been a lot of good, but there has also been much disappointment. I faced enough disappointment that I felt stuck.

Who hasn't experienced disappointment? Is there anyone whose life turns out exactly as they plan? Are we not all in this together—desperately needing to see God's joy in the midst of the disappointment? Circumstances don't work out the way that we wish they would. People let us down, not meeting our expectations. Churches and Christians disappoint us. Can it be that our disappointments are the very thing that draw us near to God? How can we embrace this life we've been given, knowing that God the Author is in the details?

"I have learned to kiss the wave that throws me against the Rock of Ages." This quote, attributed to Charles Spurgeon, has made its rounds on social media in recent years, and these words resonate with me today. For many years, infertility was the wave that tossed me around, ultimately bringing me closer God my Rock. Financial struggles and relationship challenges have done the same. We don't have to like the current "wave" that is tossing us around. However, we can be grateful when those very situations bring us closer to our Rock, Jesus Christ..

Psalm 27:13 (NKJV) says, "I would have lost heart unless I had believed that I would see the goodness of the Lord in the land of the living."

Deliberately looking at difficult situations to discover the good God is doing makes our gloomy circumstances look brighter. I haven't always done this well. In fact, I must choose to be intentional to see His goodness on my most difficult days. However, as I look back over the stories God has written with my life, I see His goodness. Being stranded and sick in Kenya was not how I envisioned my trip to Sudan. Hindsight showed me God's bright spots during a difficult week.

Do you ever hear someone who is always unsatisfied with life here on earth because they are consumed with the idea that things will be better in Heaven? Things will certainly be better in Heaven, and longing for Heaven is a good thing. After all, we were created with eternity in our hearts. However, the Psalmist says that he would have given up without believing that he would see the goodness of the Lord in his life. Psalm 33:5 (NKJV) says that "the earth is full of the goodness of the Lord." It's all around us! We can see the goodness of God right here and right now, in this place where we live, no matter what is happening.

I'm naturally a bit of a pessimist. I often feel disappointments strongly. Yet through my storms in life and throughout my long, hard waits, I have been thrown against the Rock of Ages—my God, who is the solid Rock to Whom I cling. Keep reading my story of how I'm learning to see beauty within barren places. My hope is that as you read, you will discover more of God's delightful surprises—even within your own disappointment.

In the last twenty years, I've learned to hold onto the Old Testament prophet Habakkuk's thought-provoking word picture:

"Though the fig tree does not bud and there are no grapes on the vines, though the olive crop fails and the fields produce no food, though there are no sheep in the pen and no cattle in the stalls… yet I will rejoice in the LORD, I will be joyful in God my Savior." (Habakkuk 3:17-18)

Even when we have nothing, we can still rejoice. No matter what you lack right now, this book is written for you.

CHAPTER 3

FEAR

**I sought the Lord and He answered me,
He delivered me from all my fears.**

Psalm 34:4

Tarantulas

A couple of years before traveling to Kenya, I took one year off between high school and college, and I moved to Central America to be part of a missionary training school. An 18-year-old girl who had lived a pretty easy life, I suddenly came face-to-face with one of my biggest fears during my first week in Panama.

My missionary training school consisted of about a dozen students and another dozen staff members. Most of us lived in a small cluster of buildings that included an office, sleeping quarters, a classroom, and a common living area. In that tropical climate, fresh air blew through the windows and rainstorms came hard. After a thunderstorm passed by, the greenery outdoors would sparkle, and there was always a steamy humidity in the air. When we had a Christmas party, we cut paper snowflakes out of white printer paper, and they melted. Well, they didn't quite melt, but the humidity caused them to lose their shape and hang limply from the ceiling. The electricity and running water usually worked, but they were not a guarantee. Our kitchen was simple, one of the staff members planned our menu, and our mealtimes provided a fun gathering for the entire group.

We shared the domestic duties during our time there, including cooking and cleaning. I was assigned to kitchen clean-up duty immediately, and had to learn a few things about hand washing dishes, since I had grown up with the convenience of a dishwasher.

One of my tasks included dumping the food leftovers into a compost pile in the wooded area behind our house. The woman in charge led me up a short path right behind the house, and showed me where to put the compost. She nonchalantly pointed toward some little holes in the ground, where creepy, furry arms poked out from the dirt.

"Those are the tarantula holes," she casually mentioned.

"Tarantulas?" I put on a brave face, but inside I was not okay!

I was eighteen and most certainly still scared of spiders. While growing up I would pay my younger (and more fearless) sister a quarter to kill any bugs I found in my bedroom. Spiders were creepy! And I was supposed to walk into a forest that had tarantulas crawling around? To step over the dwellings of spiders that were the size of the palm of my hand?

Despite the skin-crawling, nerve-wracking, get-me-out-of-here feelings in that first moment, this exposure to something I feared, without being harmed, eventually made me stronger. The spiders never came close to us. (Maybe they're telling tales today about how creepy the missionaries were when we invaded their land?)

I remember hearing a story from my friend Jennifer after she had become a staff member of the missions base the following year. Her bedroom was on the ground floor, and as she began to get dressed one morning, she grabbed a pair of pants off of the shelf where she stored them, and a tarantula fell onto her foot then ran away!

A tarantula on her foot as she got dressed for the day—oh my! I'm sure she didn't wear those pants that day, and I'm glad I never found a tarantula hiding in my clothes! (However, during my months in Panama, we did find bats hanging in our hall closet, and we saw scorpions clinging to our bathroom and bedroom walls.)

The things we fear can creep in close to us. How do we overcome fear?

After cohabitating with tarantulas, I've since feared little creatures much less. Well, I would say I'm no longer scared of spiders, but the basement apartment where we lived while I wrote this is occasionally visited by those insects we call "spider crickets" or "camel crickets." If you've seen them, your heart might be racing right now. If you've never seen them, imagine a bug that likes to live in cooler, damper places like caves or basement storage rooms. They look a bit like spiders but can jump several feet in the air. Their wild jumping makes them difficult to catch or kill. If you come at one of these creatures with a shoe it might jump right at you or it might jump behind the nearest piece of furniture. I might not be so scared of regular old spiders after my encounters with tarantulas, but when I'm visited by a spider cricket late at night or early in the morning I feel quite jumpy!

Five months after seeing tarantulas in the wild, I finished the missionary training school, and I went home feeling discouraged and clueless about what to do with my life. After feeling depressed at home for a few months, I returned to Panama to work throughout the summer before starting college.

Monkey Soup

Two memories from that summer are so unique that they have forever shaped my life. Since I could speak Spanish moderately then, I was invited to be a translator for another short term missions group. I would meet up with them in the city and travel around for a day of performing a dramatic presentation and talking to people about our faith. We performed and shared with people in parks and schools. After a couple of weeks, the leaders of this group invited me to spend a week with their team in the jungle.

Panama City, the capital of Panama, is not far from the Darien jungle, one of the most dense jungles in the world. There is a highway that runs from Canada to Panama that is stopped by this jungle. The teen missionary organization I was assisting had an opportunity to take a group of high schoolers into the jungle for a week to experience village life and to share our faith in Christ.

After getting permission from the leaders at my missionary base, I packed my clothes, personal supplies, some snacks, and my sleeping bag and mosquito net, and hopped onto the bus into the city. I joined up with the team I would accompany, and we boarded another bus that took us to the canoes. I remember climbing into a dugout canoe with a handful of other teenagers and traveling to our village, a place where there were no roads or electricity, and life was very different.

Was I nervous? I'm sure I was excited, but I don't remember being afraid. That week I slept in a large hut with the rest of the team, and we tried to be culturally sensitive to the local people by happily eating any meals they offered us. Our team leaders had brought some easy-to-prepare food for us to eat that week, foods like oatmeal and canned tuna. (I didn't care for either of those foods back then as a picky teenager.) We used one of the few outhouses in the village as our toilet. I took one bath that week—with my clothes on, in the river. While trying to discreetly wash with a bar of soap, it slipped out of my hand and into the murky river water. At least the bath was refreshing, even if it didn't help me smell or look any better.

Oh my, the smell. While living in Panama, I was grateful that we had access to running water and electricity most of the time. Our showers were often cold, but the water was fresh enough. A few weeks after my group's trip into the jungle, I greeted another team as they returned from their jungle week. As the crowd of teenagers exited the bus and entered the hotel lobby where we waited to greet them, their smell was overpowering. Fifty teenagers who had been sleeping on a dirt floor and bathing in a river for a week smelled an awful lot like dirt and body odor. I'm sure I smelled the same during my jungle week.

After a canoe ride into the dense jungle, we arrived at our village and set up camp in the community hut where our group slept on sleeping bags under mosquito nets. The bugs reached us anyway, and one morning I awakened to discover an insect bite near my eye that caused my face to swell. I don't really know what I looked like without access to a decent mirror. And my adventure in the jungle happened long before the invention of smart phones or selfies, so I couldn't take a picture.

Another morning as I began to wake up, I heard the other girls on the team were whispering to each other: "Where have all the guys gone?"

Looking around confirmed that early in the morning, all the males from our team had left. We soon heard that they had gone hunting with the local men. Sure enough, a couple of hours later the village men and the American teen boys returned with their catch. Hanging from a pole suspended between shoulders were two animals: a cute little dead monkey and a more unusual small animal called a jungle cat. Curiously, I followed the crowd toward a kitchen hut, and watched as they began to skin the monkey. My stomach could only handle so much, so I left mid-way through the preparation.

"They're going to eat that monkey," the teenagers whispered to each other.

Then a greater fear was realized.

"Oh no, they're going to feed *us* that monkey!"

That evening, our group heaved a corporate sigh of relief when monkey soup did not appear, and we were given tuna fish sandwiches for dinner. Suddenly tuna, a food I had never enjoyed, sounded very appealing. I was glad to know that the locals would eat their chunky monkey soup and we could eat our tuna.

However, the next day, when it was time for our noon meal, the local villagers brought a meal to our hut. We watched in dread as they carried a huge pot of soup. Monkey soup.

I wasn't eager to taste it, but we had been trained to eat whatever was set before us, out of respect for the culture we were in. Remembering this requirement, our group of western teenagers tried our best to consume our meal as to not offend those who had offered it to us.

"What did monkey taste like?" People have asked me this question for years when I've shared this tidbit.

"I have no idea," I reply. "I dumped salt into that soup and tried to swallow it, then discreetly tried to throw away as much as possible."

The summer that I encountered monkey stew, I also had another traveling adventure – this time it was not in the safety of a group visiting a jungle village – instead it was just Jennifer (the one who found a tarantula in her pants) and me. Together, two 19-year-old American girls traveled to Costa Rica fearlessly.

In Central America, you can travel from one country to the next within a day's drive. Jennifer and I had made this same trip with a group several months before. Because she was intending to stay in the country longer than I was, she was required to leave periodically to maintain her visa. She needed to leave the country for a few days, and I was up for the adventure.

Our plans for travel were approved by our missionary leaders, and I'm sure my email to my parents said something like, "We're heading to Costa Rica, I'll be back in a few days!"

At that time, dial-up internet was around, and it was primarily used for basic things like email. We didn't have Skype or Facetime, or even Google maps or Wikipedia to help us plan our trip. Was the world safer then, or did we just not know about kidnappings or sex trafficking? Were we simply more fearless in that generation, or was life safer? I do not know. We climbed aboard the bus for our eight hour ride, and headed for the border.

Upon arrival, we followed our instructions to find a certain hotel. My primary memory from this hotel is how the owner pulled the largest key ring I've ever seen out of her bra and unlocked our door for us!

After unpacking, Jennifer and I ventured out. We stayed in that town for two to three days, entertaining ourselves by attending a local church service, where we met a family who invited us to their home for a meal. We ate with them and painted our fingernails with their daughters.

One day we were walking through town and met an American man who gave us a ride in his pickup truck. (No, I wouldn't be so carefree and trusting today! I wouldn't recommend that teen girls hop into a truck with a strange man in a foreign country! I am grateful that he was trustworthy and that our guardian angels were working hard.)

During our few days in Costa Rica, Jennifer and I wandered around town, ate at restaurants, slept at our hotel, and when it was time to get our passports stamped and board our bus home, we did so.

Arriving back in our city, we met our fellow missionaries at the bus station and they drove us to our missions base. I'm sure that I emailed my parents about our adventures.

I was nineteen. I was a good kid and had some street smarts, but I was *only nineteen* when I traveled in foreign lands, eating monkey soup and hanging out with strangers in the next country over.

I was rather fearless.

CHAPTER 4

FEAR LESS

Perfect love casts out fear...

1 John 4:18 (NKJV)

If you could fast-forward life to my thirties, you'd find me married, more mature, and quite aware of all the crime and scary stuff in this world thanks to the internet and TV. You'd find me on a trip where I traveled to another part of the world, all alone. In this era, terrorist attacks were happening too frequently, at times bringing injury or death to westerners in foreign lands.

As I prepared to fly alone to visit friends, I was wrestling with something that did not haunt me as a teenager in the 90s: fear.

What was I afraid of as I traveled? Hadn't I spent a week in a jungle eating monkey soup and being bitten by insects, riding in a dugout canoe – completely trusting those who were taking me there? And now I'm afraid to fly to a strange land on an airplane? I'm an adult, I've lived alone, I can take care of myself. Why am I afraid?

Fear had crept in because I had read the news articles of planes going down – too many in recent years. I had heard of women being abducted and terrorists shooting into a crowd with no warning. Thanks to the internet, we know about all of these things. There was tension between the United States and the Middle East as I prepared for my travels, so I felt nervous.

And I was alone.

I knew how to navigate airports by myself, but I also knew that I would need to take a taxi from the airport to the bus station, where I'd buy a bus ticket, and travel for several more hours. I prepared myself to take all of these steps in a land where I did not speak the language.

A newly released worship song had caught my attention and it reminded me of my identity as a daughter of the King. I didn't have to give in to feelings of fear.

The lyrics and music words seeped into my heart, the song played on repeat as I traveled. When I took the headphones out of my ears, this song kept playing in my mind, reminding me that God who could wash away my fear and protect me as His child.

I knew that I didn't need to be mastered by fear for one moment because as a child of God I was traveling this journey with Him. Just like He parted the sea for the Israelites as they fled from Egypt, God could make my path straight and clear—and He could keep me safe as I journeyed into a foreign land that frankly felt a little scary to me.

1 John 4:18 reminds us that there is no fear in God's love—and this perfect love drives out all fear. In my life, and maybe in yours too, fear and disappointment have come hand-in-hand. Disappointment happens, and fear whispers "but what if…"

To me, fear has whispered things like "what if you never have a baby or never become a mom," or "what if you struggle financially for the rest of your lives," or "what if what if the books you write are boring and people don't like them?" Then the baby came along, and new fears followed: "what if something terrible happens to her?"

The what-ifs whispered by fear and the voice of the enemy are hard to wrestle with.

When I turn to the Word of God, He reminds me through Galatians 4:6-7 that I am a child of God. "Because you are sons, God sent the Spirit of His Son into our hearts, the Spirit who calls out 'Abba, Father.' So you are no longer a slave, but a son…'"

Whether the fear trying to sneak in is the fear of a spider or the fear that something bad is going to happen, let's understand that fear is a real thing, and fear can piggy-back on disappointment. The devil sees us feeling down and whispers "what if your worst nightmare comes true, or what if this miserable part of your life is like that forever."

I am learning to trust that God's power is greater than fear because I am His child. We can cry out to our Abba Daddy; we don't have to be ruled by fear anymore.

I navigated my flights, prayed through the turbulence over the ocean, rode in a taxi, bought a bus ticket, and made my way to visit my friends, all the while reminding myself that I am a child of God, so I don't have to move through life in fear. On my return trip, I stayed overnight in a foreign city. It occurred to me that it was the first time in my life that I would be staying in a hotel room alone. I've slept in many hotel rooms during my thirty-some years – with my family, friends, and my husband, but this was the first time I would stay all alone in another country. I checked in at the front desk, thankful that the clerk understood English sufficiently. Pulling my luggage behind me, I took my key up to my room, and stepped inside. I locked the door behind me and looked around.

Guess what greeted me in that hotel room?

A spider. Not a tiny one. A big spider was watching me from the ceiling above the bed. Although I was no longer terrified by spiders, I knew I wouldn't be able to sleep with it on the loose. I took off a shoe, stepped up onto the bed, and killed that little creature. I flushed him down the toilet for good measure, not wanting him to regain strength and climb out of the wastebasket.

Vulnerability

An even greater fear I learned to overcome in my thirties was probably the fear I battled with at age 19: the fear of being vulnerable. At 19 I could hop on a bus to another country to explore, and I could eat monkey meat in the jungle, but I was too timid to bare my soul, to be honest about my hopes and dreams, and to expose the deeper places of my heart.

Just after turning 35, I published my first book, *When Infertility Books Are Not Enough: Embracing Hope During Infertility*. While writing about my experience was therapeutic; sharing what I wrote with others was terrifying. Publishing this book was my greatest step of vulnerability at that point in my life. I wrote about my struggle to become a mother, baring my soul, opening up about my medical history, and then making it available for anyone in the world to read it. I felt like I was sharing my diary on the internet for all to see.

Through that process I learned something about taking a huge step to overcome a challenge or a fear. When recounting my monkey soup story to a friend around that time, I told her that after eating monkey soup I have been able to at least try any food, even if I really didn't like it. Every other food that has been placed before me seems easy!

She commented that publishing my first book on a topic as personal as my own infertility story, was like eating monkey soup—everything else would feel easier in comparison. After seeing tarantulas in the wild, a small spider in the house no longer bothers me like it once did. After seeing a dead monkey and tasting its meat, unusual foods don't stress me out like it used to. After vulnerably sharing my most difficult struggles, insecurity does not plague me like it did in my teens and twenties.

It's true: when you trust the Lord to take a step of overcoming fear, especially when you become vulnerable out of obedience to God, you will find that you begin to fear less. Maybe you're not completely fearless in all things, but without a doubt, the more you trust God, the more you'll overcome fear.

Fear can be so much more than fear of spiders or fear of traveling in a foreign land. We wrestle with fear of rejection. Fear of confrontation. Fear of failure. So many fears are legitimate - at first.

But we can't feed them. We must let the perfect love of our good, good Father cast out our fears.

When I went off to college just before turning 20, I would have laughingly told you about how I ate monkey soup or how I traveled by bus to another country with a friend. However, I might not have told you how, months before that, I had cried behind a mask because I had no idea what to do with my life. I might have told you the funny stuff, but I would not have been vulnerable about the ache inside me.

New Life

Not only did my international trip provide me an opportunity to overcome fear, it also helped me realize that new life can grow in unexpected places. While traveling to the hotel where that spider awaited me, I gazed out the window of my bus, crying tears over the infertility I had been experiencing for years. I saw barren plains and a desert-like land of red clay stretching out as far as my eyes could see. Bushy green plants peppered the otherwise infertile landscape.

Remembering the produce stands in the market, but looking at the desert terrain out in the distance, I asked where all of that produce came from. Berries and peppers, cucumbers and oranges overflowed the shopkeeper's stalls – how could all this vegetation grow in such a dry-looking area where olives grew naturally but berries certainly did not grow as easily? Some was brought in from farmlands, they said, where there is more fertile soil many miles away. Yet much of the produce I saw in the market was grown in greenhouses, they told me.

Pondering my own barren womb and the many people I knew longing for new life to grow within them, I was reminded that with God, all things are possible. Life can grow in that place you think is barren. (And sometimes you need the help of a greenhouse to grow new life in a barren place. Interestingly enough, when we finally decided to visit a fertility clinic, the doctor who oversaw our care was named Dr. Greenhouse. Sometimes new life needs the help of a greenhouse, and sometimes God does a miracle without the doctor's help!)

Just as life can abound within a greenhouse in the desert, it can surprise us elsewhere. Have you ever paused to ponder the beauty of life growing in unlikely places? One early summer day, I went out for a run around our local college campus near Washington, D.C., where I admired the rows of flowers that the landscapers had planted in gardens along the sidewalk. As I passed by a storm drain on the side of the road, I stopped running to look at a remarkable development (and of course, I pulled out my phone to take a picture). Inside of that storm drain, one of the plants tossed aside by a gardener had taken root, and flowers were blooming in the concrete drain. Not long after, a friend of mine shared a picture with me of a cherry tomato plant that had taken root through a crack in a parking lot – it had found enough soil and water, so there in the parking lot it was growing and bearing fruit!

Even in the most hopeless and desolate places, life can grow. In a particularly rough week during my most barren season, feeling the pain of an empty womb and the frustration over financial struggles, I was fighting feelings of despair. Preferring natural remedies over medicine, I remembered that my essential-oil-loving friends recommend frankincense to combat stress. Out of curiosity, I googled it to learn more, and while reading up on the amazing effects that frankincense can have on the body and mind, I was struck by the fact that the frankincense plant grows in rocky, barren deserts.

The very plant that grows in conditions that seem less than ideal for growth is used by some to fight depression and anxiety, and it's also known for healing the scars on a person's skin. (Remember, I am not a medical professional, I am simply telling you what I have learned from my "oily" friends.) That plant growing in a desert is evidence of the goodness of the Lord right here in the land of the living. Even in barren places, life-giving plants can grow.

A passage of Scripture that has spoken to my heart during some of the more difficult years paints another beautiful picture of God providing for us in the "dry" seasons of life:

"Blessed is the man who trusts in the Lord, and whose hope is the Lord. For he shall be like a tree planted by the waters, which spreads out its roots by the river, and will not fear when heat comes; but its leaf will be green, and will not be anxious in the year of drought…" Jeremiah 17:7-8 (NKJV) tells me that I will be blessed when I trust in the Lord and put my hope in Him, and I do not have to be anxious when I'm in a "year of drought" or a season of barrenness. Those words wash peace over my anxiety-prone soul, so I wrote them on a chalkboard a couple of years ago and haven't erased it since, allowing God's word to speak to me as I pass by the words in the entryway of my home.

As I journeyed to and from the visit to friends in a desert land, the God who parts the sea guided me to and from my destination. I felt groggy as I traveled, yet I was not alone. I was walking out this journey with my Father God who is my most faithful friend, who loves me more than my earthly parents do, and who cares about me even more than my husband does. My Father God is the one who parts every sea and washes away my fear.

I now look back on my travels as a young woman, especially my time in Panama that held many highs and lows. After a year on the mission field, I went off to college to face new challenges. I rediscovered my journal from college years recently, but I couldn't bear to read it because I was on such an emotional roller coaster in college. Though I consider those to be some tough years, in those same years I met some of my best friends and I began to know God in a fresh way.

CHAPTER 5

FRIENDSHIP

A sweet friendship refreshes the soul.

Proverbs 27:9 (The Message)

"There are some girls playing guitars and singing worship songs down here, and I think you'd like it," said my cousin, calling me on the dormitory phone.

After moving away from the tropics of Panama, I settled into a college dorm, nestled into the rolling hills of Tennessee. I attended a small Christian college that several of my family members attended over the years. Being a very small school at the time, everyone knew everyone else. If a person wasn't a friend, you at least knew of him or her. For example, a few years after graduating from college, I stopped at a traffic light on my way home from work in North Carolina. With my car windows open, I could hear the guy in the vehicle next to mine. Realizing that he was asking me a question, I looked over at him. He had seen my college bumper sticker, and he asked if I knew a buddy of his. "Yes, Dave was a classmate of mine," I replied as the light turned green. A few years after that, while living in the Washington, D.C. suburbs, I wore my college t-shirt to Wal-Mart, where an employee stopped me to ask about it. I discovered that he had attended college there with my aunt. Though it was a small school for many years, our college held a tight-knit community.

On my college campus, I found lifelong friends. These friends, along with many other friends I have made as I've moved around the country in the past couple of decades, are some of the greatest gifts of God in my life. When life brings challenges, a faithful friend is truly a demonstration of God's goodness.

One night within my first two weeks of college, my cousin called my room phone from her dorm across campus. (Yes this was back when we memorized landline phone numbers and physically dialed them.) She told me I would like the music her dorm mates were playing, so I ventured down the hill to check it out. Sure enough, fellow students were playing instruments and singing worship songs in a dorm lobby. I had already met a couple of them, but those girls then invited me to visit their church, which soon became my church as well. These girls are some of my dearest friends to this day (and we still enjoy worshipping in song together).

As an extroverted freshman, I made friends quickly, and having started college on the heels of living in Panama, I was drawn to the international community. I shared a dorm room with an exchange student from Korea and began tutoring students learning English as a second language. Although I might not have realized it at the time, what I needed after my gap year on the mission field was a secure family of brothers and sisters who would help me grow. I am so glad that I found that within the church community I plugged into.

The following summer, several of my newfound friends graduated from college and decided to rent a house together. I spent a summer there, then moved in with the girls midway through my sophomore year. An older three-bedroom red brick house on a country road was the perfect place for young women in our early twenties, trying to figure out adult life. Some of us were still in school while some worked at various jobs, and all of us went to the same church. We had our disagreements and probably even a few spats, but we bonded together. In that house where Rebekah planted one of her many amazing gardens, the five of us planted the seeds of a lifelong friendship.

Our house was the place where the young singles liked to hang out. We welcomed our friends and their friends to come over to play games, watch movies, and eat meals together. (We roasted a lot of hotdogs outdoors and ate a lot of pasta. The only foods I knew how to make back then were pasta and peanut butter fudge.) As the sun set, we would roast marshmallows over the bonfire on the edge of our gravel driveway.

We made memories as we opened our home to others. Of course, one of the reasons why we welcomed all the singles we knew was because we were wondering, "is this the one God intends for me to marry?" Yes, we were each searching for our future husbands, and come to think of it, the other girls all began dating their husbands while we lived in that house! I wasn't dating, and I felt left behind, although I can now say that my husband was worth the wait.

The Chix

Since we lived on Cherokee Road, one of the guys in our circle of friends nicknamed us the Cherokee Chix and the title stuck. Since then, the five of us have called ourselves The Chix. (However, now that we're in our forties, maybe we should start going by The Hens?)

For the first eighteen years of my life, I lived with my parents and my three biological siblings. Even though we welcomed some foster siblings for a while, and even though cousins and friends who were like family spent countless hours at our house, nobody else shares the same bond with my siblings that I do. We've added spouses into our sibling group, and although we love having them in the family, our spouses don't have the foundation of shared memories and shared upbringing that my brother and sisters and I have.

That's the way I feel about these friends I call The Chix. We have many mutual friends and know each other's families. Our involvement in each other's lives during our early twenties, those crucial growing-up years, and continued communication has deeply connected us for decades. No one can replace this five-way relationship built on shared experiences, hours of conversation, and endless emails, texts, and phone calls over the years. Currently we rely on video chats and occasional text messages to keep us connected.

I realize that not everyone has a tight-knit community of trusted friends, and that the people God has placed in my life are a tremendous gift from God. I have carried these friendships with me as I have moved around the country, and I am so grateful for them. Plenty of people have so much more in life than I do. Some of my friends and family members are better off financially, many are homeowners when I am not, and others have the houseful of children I dreamed of having. Maybe you have a newer car than me, or your body is healthier or more in shape than mine. You might have a better relationship with your parents or your spouse than I do. But it's not about comparison. I tell you about my sisterhood of treasured friends with hope that you will look around to find the goodness of God in your own life.

These Chix became my forever friends in that little brick house on Cherokee Road. I want to tell you a little bit about them because they have been foundational to who I have become as an adult. Together we have walked with God and kept each other on the right path. We have repeatedly reminded one another that God knows what He's doing, He's always good toward us, and He will lead us through every challenge that comes our way. I can't imagine life without their encouragement and prayers.

Bethany is the spunkiest one in the group. She's a free spirit, a gifted musician and writer. Listening to her play the guitar or keyboard while she sings in worship makes me want to worship God even more. I am amazed by the depth of her knowledge on so many subjects, especially when it comes to the Bible and relationships. These days you can find her leading ministries and mentoring others while pursuing God with her whole being. Listening to her dramatically tell stories makes me laugh until my stomach hurts! I remember a time when I was a college student, and we went sledding down a hill one winter day. Fearlessly, Bethany decided to ride her sled standing up, and she slammed right into the fence at the bottom of the hill. She was unfazed because she's tenacious like that! She and I both have strong personalities, yet we are very different from each other. We've learned to not fight over our differences, but to instead accept these variances, and often we have referred to our friendship as "iron sharpening iron," referencing the book of Proverbs. Because we've learned from each other, welcomed feedback from each other, and not let our differences build a wedge between us, we have both become better people.

Brandy is the mama of the group, whether or not she likes me giving her that title. Way back when we first met, she was a Resident Assistant in the dorm where I first lived. (An R.A. is the more mature person that college students need to keep order in the dorm.) A school-teacher-in-training at the time, she became the first among us to marry, the first to have children, and she has the most children of all the Chix. She homeschools her six children and is an example of how to love a family well. Out of all of us, I think that Brandy is most like me in personality, except she is much more organized! Her life is orderly, while I let my creative side explode into a messy home and a messy desk! Though similar in some ways, our lives have been vastly different. She married young, and her family grew rapidly while I took a while to find a spouse and struggled to have babies. I am forever grateful for the way she has cheered me on as I began writing about infertility, and I'm thankful for the way she has prayed for me and loved me.

Rebekah might appear to have a mellow personality, but her spunk and hilarity might take you by surprise. She also carries a depth of insight and speaks wisdom. In recent years she has worn more hats than I can imagine trying to keep up with: homeschooler of her three children, a part-time nurse, a part-time graphic designer, a pastor's wife, an impressive gardener, and an artist. Sometimes you'll find her tutoring other homeschoolers, teaching classes, and leading ministries. On top of that, she plays the guitar and the drums. In our twenties, she was a regular drummer on the church worship team. Rebekah is a gift. She is a powerful woman of strength and grace. She hears from God and influences more lives than she realizes.

Julie is amazing. My first impression of her was that she was fun-loving and a little boy-crazy, and living in the same dorm, I guess that felt a little like competition as we searched our small campus for husbands. (I'll admit, I think that she was more cute and more fun than me, and of course, she got married first!) As I have gotten to know Julie over the years, she's still fun, but she is also a deep well of wisdom. She has set an amazing example to me of what it means to follow God's voice, to faithfully love your husband, and how to raise lots of babies and mother them well. Julie homeschools her five children, tutors English students online, is a devoted intercessor, and has been a kindred spirit that I couldn't live without.

Marriage

I've been reflecting on the days when we were all fresh out of college and wanting to be married. Julie described it best: back then it was as if all our single guy friends had a question mark hovering over their heads. We, the single ladies, would gaze at the imaginary hovering question marks, wondering if THIS was the husband for me? As it is with twenty-something drama, some of us ruled some others out quickly, and wondered about others for a long time. Maybe guys were seeing question marks over our heads as well?

Very few of us dated within our circle of friends, although we spent countless hours together as friends, as brothers and sisters, often connected through church activities. We ate together, hiked together, played games together, took road trips together, worshipped together, and at times got on each other's nerves. Okay, I was the one getting on people's nerves with my love for practical jokes.

Then, one by one, or should I say, two by two, people began having lightbulb moments from Heaven, suddenly knowing which one of those question marks was now a great big flashing star.

"This is the one for you!" God would loudly and clearly announce. Well, maybe it didn't go quite like that, but it seemed that way to me as I watched friend after friend begin dating (or courting), soon followed by engagement, then marriage just a few months later. I attended bridal showers, participated in weddings, celebrated with my friends, and as they began to transition from newlyweds to parents, I felt like the last one standing. I wasn't the only single person, but I had examined all the question marks to the point that I felt like I needed move on. I relocated to North Carolina, and eighteen months later I married Mike. (What can I say, that strategy worked for me!)

When I was in a brief (and shallow) relationship prior to meeting my husband, my mom asked me a specific question: "Will this guy be the husband to you that the Chix' husbands are to their wives?" These friends-turned-brothers had set a standard of what a God-honoring marriage looked like. Before they were husbands, these men were good, honoring friends to the women around them. (Oh, and the answer to my mom's question was no. So I dumped the guy.)

Julie's husband, Matthew, said it best, back when we were all single. "I want to look back on these days to see a trail of friends, not a trail of broken hearts." His desire during his years of dating and searching for his spouse was to honor others. Many people don't want to still be friends with an ex. But when you walk in honor toward each other, it's possible.

Matthew said the same thing to me again recently when we were talking about how important it is to have reconciliation after friendships have been broken. We were both seeing the value of reconnecting with friendships we had lost. I think it applies to all types of relationships: when we honor others we can leave behind a trail of friendship instead of heartbreak.

A few years ago, I attended a reunion with the Chix and their families. We gathered together for a meal, now as husbands and wives, with lots of children running around, I thought about how grateful I am for these sisters and brothers. We can get together and hang out and feel thankful for each other because we honored one another when we were young, even though we had moments of tension, we had disagreements, and sometimes we had enough of each other.

When you choose to do life with someone—whether it be the everyday mundane of sharing a house and cleaning it together or the deeper moments of prayer and worship, whether you're supporting each other in prayer and encouragement through the ups and downs of life, if you honor the people in your life, you're going to have treasured friends down the road.

This speaks to marriage as well – persevering through the difficult times, sharing life experiences together, sharing a home, and praying together – all of these things build a relationship. When you choose to honor the other person throughout, you'll have a treasured friend as a spouse, not a broken hearted one.

My Chix friendships began on a college campus, blossomed in a little brick house on Cherokee Road, and walked together into marriage and motherhood. Eventually several of us began to move away from Tennessee, keeping in touch across the miles. Finally, fifteen years after our lives merged in that little brick house, we planned a girls' weekend.

A flurry of emails and texts carried on for weeks as we tried to nail down a date for our girls' weekend, planning to meet in Nashville, Tennessee. We would be driving in from four states. I was the only one without children, although I worked full-time as a nanny. I requested time off work, and the other Chix searched their calendars for a weekend that would work for their husbands to care for their children. Finally, we chose a weekend in June and booked a hotel.

Not long before the weekend arrived, I asked the Chix if they realized that we had inadvertently planned our weekend for Father's Day. More than a dozen children between the four of them, left with their husbands for a girls' getaway on Father's Day weekend. Oops!

CHAPTER 6

PAIN AND HEALING

Perfect submission, all is at rest;
I in my Savior am happy and blessed,
watching and waiting, looking above,
filled with His goodness, lost in His love.

Fanny J. Crosby, hymnwriter

Not long before the girls' weekend, I began experiencing severe pain. It all began in March. Actually, it probably started before then, but March of that year was a turning point. When our huge health insurance deductible started over, Mike and I decided to once again pursue medical intervention as we attempted to start our family. Since I'll be talking about health and healing, I must remind you that I am not a medical professional, I am not giving medical advice in this book, I am simply telling my story.

Around the beginning of that year, I went to my doctor to start considering our reproductive options once again. We had done this other years, and taken a break some years, because fertility treatments were so expensive. So in the first week of March, I went to my doctor's office for an uncomfortable procedure, and she determined that we should operate to remove some growths that could be hindering pregnancy.

I walked into the office of the woman who scheduled surgery at my clinic. "How soon can I schedule this procedure?" I asked, knowing that my doctor only operates at the hospital two days of the month. With some discussion, we reviewed calendars and scheduled the surgery for just a couple of weeks later, March 17.

The week of surgery I publicly asked our Facebook friends for prayer. "Our faith in God's ability to fill this empty womb after so many years is strong. Without a doubt, we know that God knows what's going on, that His timing is right, and we truly believe that He has children for us. We're not giving up any time soon, but we feel a real peace and confirmation from Him that He's able to bring that breakthrough very soon."

The surgery went well, I recovered quickly, and the next couple of months passed by without resulting in pregnancy. *What else can I do?* I wondered. I had heard that chiropractic care could help boost fertility. My insurance will pay for it so why not give it a try? I scheduled an appointment with a chiropractor, explaining it him that I had heard it might benefit my fertility, and I also described some minor aches and pains in my back.

Unfortunately, my first adjustment by the chiropractor triggered a severe headache that also caused my neck and back to hurt so much that I could barely function. I cancelled follow up appointments, because I was afraid it would become worse. The immobilizing pain I often felt in the days ahead took fear to a whole new level. I might have gotten over a fear of spiders, and I might have begun to realize that God was with me and I had nothing to fear while traveling alone. But new thoughts crept into my mind and made their home there: *What if this pain never goes away? What if I've been permanently damaged? What if this pain will haunt me every day for the rest of my life?* I know many people deal with chronic pain, and I feared it.

My head, neck, and upper back hurt tremendously, especially when I climbed out of bed in the mornings. The back of my neck throbbed as I transitioned from lying down to standing upright. I began each day with pain relievers, a hot shower, and a desperate prayer. Sometimes I would wake up and get dressed, then simply sit on the couch with an ice pack on my neck. My anxiety level skyrocketed and I felt like a fool for randomly choosing this chiropractor. My thoughts felt condemning. *It was my fault for even going there. I've brought this onto myself.*

I sought prayer from friends and family. I took prescribed muscle relaxers and over-the-counter painkillers. I tried to rest and I took naps. I tried to pray, but this new fear called "what if" tormented me.

Not only was my neck hurting, but I was experiencing a painful inflammation in my hip and it hurt to walk, climb stairs, or sit for long periods. After a few weeks, I went to a primary care doctor who said the hip pain would go away on its own, and she called the pain in my neck "muscle spasms" and suggested muscle relaxers. I walked out of her office feeling assured that I was not permanently damaged and I was not going to die.

This might sound as if I'm overreacting, but have you ever experienced pain so severe that you fear the worst? When our bodies are in severe pain, it's easy for our minds to run wild. Fear creeps in and gains a foothold. My fear of "is it always going to be like this?" was much bigger and uglier than the creepy feeling I had when I saw tarantulas in Panama. Without a doubt the enemy of our souls wants to get us down, and he is willing to attack our bodies in the process.

I want to pause for one moment to say that many people I know have had good results from going to a chiropractor. I have nothing against chiropractors, I simply had a bad reaction and my pain kept me from walking back through those doors again.

However, while experiencing this pain, I was reminded of what God did for me in the past. Just like overcoming smaller fears helps us to be stronger in the future, I can look at God's healing power in my past and trust that He's able to heal me now, and in the future.

Often Christians turn to medicine first, and sometimes don't even pray about their health problems. God is continually teaching me about His healing power. He's the one who designed our bodies, and He's the one who can fix them! I'm not against seeking medical care and I am not one to advocate only prayer and never medicine. There is room for both.

I've Seen God Heal

When I was first exposed to healing ministries as a teenager on mission trips, sometimes the minister would pray for someone, then ask the person for a testimony and the person would say that her pain was totally gone! I would wonder if healing really happened. How could she know so soon that she was actually healed? I was a bit of a skeptic.

Then in my later teens and throughout my twenties, I had a lot of headaches. Unfortunately, headaches and migraines run in both sides of my family, and I first went to the doctor with headaches when I was in elementary school. But around the time I married in 2008, I was having an average of six or eight migraines or severe headaches each month. They were so frequent that I remember specifically praying that I would not have a migraine on my wedding day. (I didn't, thank God!)

I learned to avoid migraine triggers like caffeine, certain foods or smells, and I tried several prescription medications. Not long after we were married, I made an appointment with a neurologist who specialized in headaches and migraines. Even after following her protocol, the migraines eased up a little bit, but they continued to torment me.

For years we prayed that God would take away my headaches. A friend was praying diligently for me to have relief. Once we were married, Mike began to pray daily that I would not have headaches. He has continued to pray this for years.

Our prayers are never wasted, but when I continually asked God to heal these headaches and I didn't experience any changes, I began to wonder, "God didn't heal me last time, why would he heal me if I ask for prayer this time?"

We continued to ask God for breakthrough in my chronic

headaches and migraines. One year after we were married, at two separate Christian meetings, I received specific prayer for breakthrough. At the time, I was keeping a record of how frequently I experienced headaches, and after those two specific times of prayer, the migraines slowed down, and eventually faded away. Since then, on rare occasions I have a moderate headache.

It took me about a year from the time of prayer to feel confident that I was truly healed from the migraines. I gave it time, and my healing was for real.

Pain Can Trigger Fear

Years later, when I faced severe pain once again because of my chiropractor experience, I had to remind myself that God had healed me in the past. He could do it again. Although the pain in my hip faded, my upper back and neck continued to experience unusual pain. I feared that I would always suffer from this pain. When thoughts tormented me, I learned how to say "shut up, Satan" with the same fervency I would use to command a poorly behaved dog lunging toward me when walking through my neighborhood. The devil certainly wants to get us down, and he succeeds sometimes. He saw that I had overcome some fears, so he threw new ones in my direction.

Your fears might look different from mine. For me, it used to be spiders. For you, it might be snakes. While writing this, I lived in a basement apartment, and from the very week we moved in, we found small garden snakes hanging out in our entryway during warm weather.

At first, I would fearfully jump over a little snake on the sidewalk as quickly as possible as I walked out the door. I would text my husband, asking him to move the snake into the grass. Back then, a garden snake would send a shiver down my spine, even if it was no bigger than a pencil. In case you're thinking that we should have put them to death, we didn't kill those harmless little guys.

Then I started to get used to seeing an occasional snake outside my door. I'd just step over it and move along. One Saturday morning when Mike was in the shower, I opened the door to see what the outdoor temperature felt like before selecting my clothes for the day.

Plop!

I heard it, and from the corner of my eye, I saw it fall.

A snake had somehow climbed onto the door, and as I opened the door into the house, the little creature fell into the entryway of our home. My husband was unable to rescue me, and I had to do something. Quickly I reached for a dustpan, scooped up the snake, and threw him out into the yard.

When you boldly confront your fears over and over again, they become less intimidating and you can just throw them out the door. New fears might try to sneak in, but in the process of trusting God, we become stronger.

Pain and fear were so intertwined for me that summer, set off by the chiropractor then following me on my girls' weekend to Nashville.

The day I was to start my drive from my home in the Washington, D.C. suburbs to the rolling hills of Tennessee, I called my husband, wondering if I could press through the pain and make it to my destination. I wanted to spend time with these dear sisters, the Chix, and I decided to press on. With an ice pack on the tense muscle of my upper back, I began the drive to Tennessee.

Fear haunted me that night. As the sky grew dark, a terrible thunderstorm swept through, tearing branches from trees and making the car feel as if it was being blown around by the wind. Thankfully, that stretch of interstate is one I am very familiar with, having driven back and forth between my childhood home and my college town countless times.

I debated whether to pull over and wait out the storm or to press through. I kept driving, praying for safety and rebuking fear as I drove. I called my husband on my hands-free device to ask him to pray as well. I followed large trucks in front of me, hoping they would forge a path in case there was any debris blown in from the rainstorm. Trees had fallen on the sides of the road, but the street remained clear. My car seemed to be making a funny sound, and I was terrified of breaking down on the side of the road late at night in a thunderstorm.

Pain can trigger fear. What began with "am I going to feel this pain for the rest of my life" quickly led to "not only am I in pain, but now I'm going to be in pain and stranded on the side of the road in the darkness during a thunderstorm!"

I traveled to Nashville with my dear friends, where we spent 48 hours talking, praying, painting our nails, and mindlessly coloring the patterns and floral designs in adult coloring books. These friends have walked with me through the good and the bad for nearly twenty years, and our prayers for each other keep us going.

The Body of Christ

Months after our Nashville weekend, one of the Chix emailed me a large sad face emoji with the words, "I have been praying so often for your womb!" She was responding to my disappointing news that I was still not pregnant, despite medical intervention. Though it might seem strange to pray for a person's uterus or reproductive system, I was so grateful that people prayed me through years of struggling to become pregnant.

While typing this chapter, I wrote a text message to a friend of mine who is battling chronic health problems. "I want God to break through in your health!" said my message, and I realized that I was seeing the body of Christ at work. This is the healing of bodies within The Body—we need others to pray for us that we might be healed. Praying for one another and having faith and hope for each other are vital. The Scripture says for us to "bear one another's burdens." It also describes Christ Jesus as the one who bears our burdens. I might feel discouraged about my own health struggles, but I can still pray with faith for someone else.

After about six weeks of almost daily back and neck pain following that chiropractor visit, knowing that I didn't want to continue relying on muscle relaxers, I felt God prompting me to go to a Physical Therapist (P.T.) I had never been a patient at a physical therapy office before, but I knew of a Christian woman whom I felt like I could trust with my pain.

That's one of the struggles people might have when praying for healing—we feel so embarrassed to explain our situation or to ask for prayer. It feels awkward at first to ask someone to pray for your reproductive system. I felt ashamed and stupid to be needing medical care. After all, I had been fine and then my body was jolted into severe pain, and I felt like it was my fault.

The first day I walked into the P.T. office, I explained that I had gone to a chiropractor which had triggered headaches, neck pain, and upper back pain. The reason I had gone to a chiropractor in the first place was to investigate whether they could help me with fertility problems. I felt like a fool, and I was in pain. I poured out my story.

She began to assess my situation, explaining that our the human body is intricately intertwined and the pain in various areas could be related. She was a voice of encouragement to me as I shared my struggle with infertility. Because of our shared faith, we could discuss spiritual principles throughout our regular appointments. We talked about how God created the body to work together, and He created the Body of Christ to work together. She used her hands to help heal my pain, knowing our hands can be used for healing because Jesus laid His hands to heal. As this Physical Therapist helped ease the pain, I began to relax, thinking, *Okay, I am not permanently damaged.*

Psalm 139 describes how intricately God knows us. He knows each of our thoughts before they pass through our minds. God has written out each day of our life in His book before the day even begins. He says that our bodies are fearfully and wonderfully made, and that He is the one who wove my body together while I was in my mother's womb.

God knew ahead of time that I would experience pain that summer. He knew that I felt like a mess of pain and infertility. He knew how to fix it. I am often reminded of God's goodness when He demonstrates His care for our bodies and our health issues, such as His care in telling a certain woman's story in the New Testament.

Jesus Cares

One morning as I read the story of Jesus healing the woman with the issue of blood, it brought tears to my eyes. I am so grateful that God included that specific miracle in His written story. As a woman who has experienced infertility, endometriosis, and painful periods, I am grateful that Jesus cared so much about the woman who was bleeding.

The woman who had been bleeding for twelve years, who desperately reached out to Jesus as He walked by, must have felt more than awkward when Jesus asked, "Who touched me?" Jesus told the crowd that He had felt power go out of Him, and this woman simultaneously felt healing in her body. She confessed that she had reached out to touch the hem of His garment, then her story became history. When you're desperate for healing, you're more likely to try something that feels uncomfortable.

Attempting chiropractic care and then physical therapy was one of the desperate attempts I've made seeking healing for my body. My P.T. reminded me that a human body is intertwined from head to toe. Pain in one area can be connected to pain in another part of the body.

As she explained this, I was reminded of 1 Corinthians 12, where Paul compares the human body to the body of Christ, demonstrating that they are both interconnected. If one part of our body is suffering, other parts of the body feel it.

Christians are connected to each other. When one is grieving, others should feel that grief. When one is rejoicing, we should share in that joy. When another Christian offends us, we shouldn't just cut them off, we should seek healing for the entire body. Romans 12 also admonishes us that since as Christians we form one body, we should work together as if we were all interconnected.

Jesus' hands were often reaching out to heal people's afflictions and demonstrating that there is power in touch. Whether it's the bleeding woman reaching out to touch Jesus, or a parent comforting a child who is crying because of a boo-boo, our hands can offer comfort and healing. Jesus reached out His hands to touch those who were sick and hurting, and they were healed. We are to be imitators of Christ, using our hands to comfort, heal, and bring God the glory.

Gradually, the pain I experienced that summer faded away, thanks to God answering my prayers and thanks to the care of a Physical Therapist. I learned strategies for easing tension in my neck and back before it worsens. Once again, God reminded me that He is our Healer. He answers prayer, and He loves to do more than we ask or imagine.

CHAPTER 7

LOST AND FOUND

**Now to Him who is able to do exceedingly abundantly
above all that we ask or think... to Him be glory...**

Ephesians 3:20-21 (NKJV)

Keys

God showers His children with delightful surprises all the time. Like the Psalmist who wrote that he knew he would see the goodness of the Lord in his life here on earth, often we simply need to open our eyes and see it. By taking note of the small gifts God gives us, we will develop an awareness of the beauty of His goodness.

Psalm 33:5 says that "the earth is full of the goodness of the Lord." (NKJV) God's delightful surprises happen more than I probably notice. The year that I began to choose to look for His divine appointments within my disappointment, God kept surprising me with unique scenarios.

One morning my alarm awakened me before the sun came up, and after making sure that the rain had not yet started, I made some coffee and changed into my running clothes, not realizing what an impact that particular morning would have on me. I felt determined to get back to my morning running routine. Running is hard, but tackling a couple of miles first thing reminds me that by the grace of God I can handle whatever else comes next. Starting my day with worship music and prayer while I push my body sets a good tone for what is to come! Sometimes those days are ordinary, and sometimes they hold miracles.

After running two miles, I returned home with just enough time to stretch, shower, and head to work. As I approached my door, I discovered that my house keys were not in my pocket although I remembered zipping them in at the beginning of my workout. Later I discovered the hole in my pocket. Thankfully, my husband was home, so I was able to get back inside. I quickly got ready to go, and decided to drive through my running route on my way to work, hoping I would find the keys in the street.

As I drove slowly through the neighborhood, I prayed, asking God to help me find my keys, and asking Him to restore what had been lost. My prayers that morning were bigger than just finding an old keychain with two house keys and a gym pass; my prayers were that God would restore lost time. I also prayed for marriages to be restored, and for empty wombs to carry life.

The Scripture from Joel 2:25 floated through my mind as I remembered that God told His people that He would restore the years that the locusts had eaten. A scene in the *Little House on the Prairie* books describes the locusts swarming in and destroying every plant in sight, wreaking havoc and causing the homesteaders to be forced to start over. Only God the Creator can restore what has been lost or even destroyed. Psalm 90:15 says, "Make us glad for as many days as You have afflicted us, for as many years as we have seen trouble." This Scripture was a prayer of Moses, a man who certainly saw affliction: Taken from his family as an infant. Fleeing to live in the wilderness for a while. Being called by God to go back to Egypt to lead an entire people group to freedom. Then Moses and all those people wandered around and around the wilderness before God ushered them into the Promised Land. There are so many more stories within that summary, but Moses prayed, "God, for as many days and years that we've experienced affliction, make us glad." (That's my paraphrase of the passage.)

This God who loves to demonstrate His goodness wants me to see beauty in barren places. He wants me to see His appointments within my disappointment. Like Moses, I want God to pour out blessings where there have been hardships.

That morning after looking for my keys, I drove on to work, arriving around 8:00. Sometime that morning I posted about the missing keys in our neighborhood Facebook group, hoping that the right person would see my post and find my keys somewhere along the miles of roadway I had covered that morning.

At 8:30 that morning I answered a phone call from my mom, who was hundreds of miles away.

"Betsy, I know you're busy right now, but I'm in my car, and I just reached into the seat pocket behind me and found your car key."

Four months earlier we had visited my parents, and it was the last place where my husband and I had seen both sets of keys to our other car. The Saab car key and key fob aren't as easy to replace or as inexpensive as an average house key, and after searching everywhere we knew to look, we had decided to manage with just one key.

But God had not forgotten.

The morning I prayed for keys to be found, for lost things to be returned, instead of spotting my house keys in the road, God let my mother find our missing car key, even within minutes of my prayer!

This was not a coincidence.

Found

Often I pray when searching for misplaced items: library books, items of clothing, everyday things that get lost in a home. Even though God usually helps me find what is lost, I'll admit that I don't always remember to acknowledge Him and thank Him. However, He sure grabbed my attention on the day of the lost keys.

Hours later, after my mom discovered the car key, I saw a response to my Facebook post. A man had been out for a walk, and he had picked up the keys. His reply described that he had hung them on a sign at a specific intersection. My husband went to retrieve them, and they were just where the man said they would be.

Less than twelve hours after losing my house keys and asking God to intervene, my Provider returned two sets of keys. God clearly demonstrated to me that He is able to answer our prayers—sometimes slowly, and sometimes quickly. He's able to give a double portion, even when we don't expect it. God doesn't forget our prayers, and even when we stop praying about something He can surprise us with an answer.

It happened again, just after Christmas the following year. (Since we usually travel to three different homes over our Christmas break, it's easy to misplace things!) Upon returning home from our whirlwind travels, I realized that I had misplaced two credit cards: one for a clothing store and the other was our everyday card. After checking the accounts online to make sure that the cards weren't being used by someone else, we decided to just keep looking around for them.

Once again, my mom contacted me one morning. "I just found your credit card in my car." (Yes, I see a trend here.) I was in the minivan that I drive for my nanny job when her text arrived. Before I got out of the van that morning, I turned around to pick up some trash from the floor, and could see down the crack between the driver's seat and the console. There was my other missing credit card. God sometimes pours out a double portion of blessings just because He can. Sometimes He returns not just one lost item, but two.

I'm sure it sounds like I lose a lot of stuff. I even lost my wedding band one Christmas Eve, as I darted through a sudden rain shower to get back to my husband's childhood home. One of my unintentional Christmas traditions has been mailing our Christmas cards just in time to be postmarked by Christmas, and I often find myself walking from my in-laws' home to the post office a day or two before the holiday. When I walked into the house after a Christmas Eve rain shower and discovered that my wedding ring was not in my pocket where I had safely tucked it, I panicked, then prayed. God, in His kindness, led me as I retraced my steps right to the spot where I had pulled something else out of my pocket and the ring had fallen to the sidewalk.

I lose precious or necessary items sometimes. Considering that while writing this I was often on the go as a full-time nanny, rarely at my house for an entire day, it was easy enough to misplace things like keys or credit cards. I think that God probably smiles when I ask for His help, and He points me to the lost thing. I certainly smile when He returns two lost sets of keys or two credit cards instead of one.

I want God to be the one who holds the keys to my life, to the opportunities before me, because His ways are so much better.

More Than We Ask or Imagine

Ephesians 3:20-21 describes God like this: "Now to Him who is able to do exceedingly abundantly above all that we ask or think… to Him be glory…" (NKJV) The NIV says "more than we ask or imagine." God likes to do exceedingly abundantly more than we can ask or imagine. On one hand I seem to only expect God to give me the bare minimum of what I need, but on the other hand, I sure can dream up a lot of things—and to know that God is able to exceed my imagination with even greater things? Wow.

God poured out blessings in fun ways when Mike and I made a major move several years ago. With much prayer and thought, we decided to move from our home in North Carolina, where we were near to many family members. We left stable jobs and friends for my husband to go to graduate school, with plans of working for the government. We agreed that it was the right time and place for me to transition to a job in full-time childcare instead of working in a cubicle. We planned it as a stepping stone toward my dream of being a stay-at-home mom.

Well, before I left my cubicle job, God allowed me to work part time for the last year. I worked the best office hours ever: I arrived at work at 10:30 in the morning and left at 2:30 in the afternoon. I came to work after everyone else and was the first to go home. This was a part-time job with benefits, a job that paid well, and working hours that were truly hard to beat.

One morning, a month before our move, Mike and I went to breakfast at our local Chick-fil-A. It was the restaurant's annual Cow Appreciation Day, the day when this chicken fast-food eatery encourages their customers to dress up like their mascot, the cow. Anyone who dresses like a cow receives a free meal, and well, we love eating free Chick-fil-A meals. Each year I take some black construction paper or felt and attach homemade cow ears to a headband, and because we attend this event annually, we have our cow t-shirts hanging in our closet. Old white t-shirts with black spots await our annual celebration of cows and chickens. On that sunny morning, Mike and I might have looked a little silly donning our cow ears and spotted t-shirts, but we enjoyed our free chicken breakfast before heading to work.

I had a few minutes at home before I needed to clock in, so I killed time in one of my favorite ways: I logged into Facebook. The

Chick-fil-A restaurant that we had just left had been running an online promotion for weeks—they would place their cow mascot somewhere around our town and then post a picture on Facebook. The first person to guess the location correctly would win a free meal.

When I pulled up Facebook on my computer, I saw the picture of the little stuffed cow sitting outside of a building. Immediately I recognized the location. I quickly typed in the name of the art museum into the comments. I couldn't believe that I was first! I had won!

I don't share this story with you to tell you that I won a free meal. Since it was Cow Appreciation Day, the restaurant was being extremely generous, and they awarded the winner that day with a year's supply of Chick-fil-A. They gave me 52 coupons for free meals! You might be able to say this was simply being on the right Facebook post at the right time, but without a doubt, this was a gift from God. He knew that Mike and I were about to take a major cut to our income. He knew that date nights would need to be cheaper. God knew that this would make us smile, and He provided hundreds of dollars for us to enjoy free date nights during the financially tight years of graduate school.

Each summer since then, I've gathered everyone close to me— my husband and now our daughter, my friends, the children I nannied for several years—together we go to Chick-fil-A on that silly Cow Appreciation Day, with black felt spots pinned to our white shirts, or white spots taped to our black shirts. I have a collection of "cow ears" made from felt, and if someone is feeling really bold, she'll pin one of my homemade cow tails to her backside. We dress up like cows in exchange for free food during that annual event.

When I don my cow costume, I find myself humming an old hymn. "Here I raise my Ebenezer, hither by Thy help I've come." Those lyrics from "Come Thou Fount of Every Blessing" by Robert Robinson[1], refer to a passage in Scripture. 1 Samuel 7:12 (NIV) says, "Then Samuel took a stone and set it up between Mizpah and Shen. He named it Ebenezer, saying, 'Thus far the Lord has helped us.'"

Ebenezer reminds us that "thus far, the Lord has helped us." When I go back to that place and remember that day when God abundantly provided meals for us, I sing about Ebenezers, these simple yet profound reminders that so far, God has helped us. Thus far, God has provided for us.

I can think of countless other ways God has provided for my husband and me. God has provided vehicles during years when our income was on the lower side, and just the right home as we have moved around due to job changes. God has given us what we need, and He's given us above and beyond what we've hoped. I still lose things that I never find again. I definitely don't win all of the drawings I enter. I live a life full of daily challenges and frustrations. I've experienced disappointment and lack. Yet throughout it all, so much has been found. Our faith has grown. God has provided for our every need in surprising ways.

Thankfulness

The stories I tell might seem simple, with topics such as finding missing keys and receiving extravagant and unexpected gifts. However,

God is working in countless ways, both big and small, in your life and mine. I encourage you to reflect on ways that He has demonstrated goodness. Tell others of the good things God has done in your life.

How has God provided for you? What prayers has He answered? Thank Him for the little things. How has He provided for your needs? When we pause to contemplate what He has done, we become more thankful to the Giver of all good and perfect gifts. We see His goodness.

1 Thessalonians 5:16-18 says, "Rejoice always, pray continually, give thanks in all circumstances; for this is God's will for you in Christ Jesus." Let's thank God for all that He does. Let's thank God for our hardships as well as the easier times. He is good all of the time, even when we can't see it.

CHAPTER 8

FOG

**Occasionally, weep deeply over the life you hoped would be.
Grieve the losses. Then wash your face. Trust God.
And embrace the life you have.**

John Piper

After reading a quote shared on Facebook, I turned to Google to find out in which book it was written. I was surprised to find that this bit of wisdom came from a tweet. Although it may have come from his other writings first, I was grateful to have discovered these words through social media, because they sure do apply to my life.

These words by John Piper have resurfaced online many times while I've been putting together this manuscript: "Occasionally, weep deeply over the life you hoped would be. Grieve the losses. Then wash your face. Trust God. And embrace the life you have." [1]

I certainly want to heed this advice to weep over my lost hopes.

Years ago, I dreamed of marrying right after college and starting a family soon after. Instead, I met my husband just after turning 28 and married him just before I turned 29. We've been happily married for more than a decade so far, but we've certainly had hardships. My simple dreams of living in a house and taking care of my children while my husband works at a fulfilling job have not come as quickly or as easily as I thought they would. I wrote the bulk of this book in my late thirties, while grieving from the years of infertility we were experiencing.

I need to be reminded to grieve, then to move forward, trusting my God. My dreams were simple (all I wanted was to be a wife and mom), and these dreams didn't come to pass when and how I thought they would.

How many others share a similar dream and feel a deep ache in their hearts when those dreams don't come true? What about more complex dreams—those who want to pursue careers that require years of training but those years are filled with struggle, struggle, and more struggle. What about those whose spouses die at a young age and their hopes of a happy life together are instead filled with an empty ache? So many people feel stuck in a rut in their jobs, wishing that life could be more fulfilling. A friend who has also struggled with making ends meet financially reminded me that most people must work hard at their finances. Even the people who look like they've got plenty of money are probably either secretly struggling or working really hard for their lifestyle. For many of us—most of us—life is full of challenges and unmet longings.

When things don't go according to our plans or even according to our hopes, we can grieve a little, then move forward with our eyes fixed on our God who created us and loves us.

How can I fully live this life that He has given me? It's hard to do that when I'm battling disappointment. There are many resources and books available on living life to the fullest. My life might not look exciting: at the moment I've grabbed a quiet moment to sit in the grass on a spring day, writing on my laptop. However, most of my days are filled with work—when I began writing this book, my week days as a nanny were filled with hour upon hour of tending to the needs of four children, their home, and three dogs. During those years, when I had time in my own home, there was a husband to spend time with, laundry to be done, and an apartment to clean, as well as a body that needed sleep, exercise, and nutritious choices to maintain this life of working and writing. As I'm finishing this book, many things have changed— same husband, different house, and instead of taking care of another couple's children, I'm at home tending to my own toddler, wondering if this is the full life Jesus promised? This life is busy and messy and overall good, but I find myself stunned by how much of my time and energy one little child can consume! Yet God shows up in the midst of my mundane days and He's there in my disappointing endeavors. His surprises make pressing on to live fully completely worth it.

Disappointment can hit us hard and fast, knocking the wind out of us. Or it can creep in and hover over us like a fog, making a person feel like they're slowly suffocating. I've felt both types of disappointment.

Though I've felt each one more than once, two specific times stand out in my mind: Easter and Christmas. Two of the most celebrated days in the Christian faith have also been tied to moments of deep disappointment for me.

Foggy Mountains

For many years my grandparents had a home in Montreat, a community nestled in the mountains of North Carolina. They served as missionaries overseas and lived in this home when they were in the United States, then settled there after retirement.

Several years later, after my grandfather passed away, my grandmother moved into a retirement home. Their house became available for our family to use for a number of years. From childhood through my early adulthood, this place was one of my favorite places to get away. Montreat, derived from the words "mountain retreat" is just that.

In the center of this place too small to be called a town, you'll find a general store that my cousins and siblings and I regularly walked to in order to buy candy. In the same building where we purchased candy, we would also spend time browsing a bookstore. We'd step outside of the shops to watch the ducks and swans in Lake Susan. Sometimes we'd ride paddle boats, or try to catch a few fish. The lake is fed by mountain streams, and we loved wading and rock hopping through the cold, refreshing mountain water.

I love to soak up the beauty of the forests, to feel the fresh mountain air, and to savor the peace found in nature. I've traveled the world, but this corner of the North Carolina mountains is one of my favorite places.

My grandparents' former home is filled with memories made with family and friends. The windows of that white A-framed house looked out into the yard and driveway, often filled with family at our reunions. The upstairs bathroom had a claw-foot bathtub that was perfect for bubble baths.

The living room's large picture window came with a warning from my grandma the first time my sisters and cousins and I held a girls' weekend there. "Don't run nikki in front of the window!" she admonished us, much to our amusement, since "running nikki" was her way of saying "running naked." With a chuckle we replied, "Don't worry, Grandmom, we won't!"

If those wood paneled walls could talk, they would speak in both English and Korean. Those walls would tell stories shared by my grandparents who had dedicated their lives to share the gospel in South Korea. The dark stairway would tell you that my cousins and siblings and I would sneak out of bed to listen to our parents' conversations at night. The upstairs bedroom is where the children slept the night my grandfather passed away in the hospital after battling an illness.

That home was filled with memories and peace. On most of our visits there, we trekked up to the highest peak in the Eastern United States. Mount Mitchell can be accessed from the Blue Ridge Parkway, and our family enjoyed hiking to the peak from the base of Greybeard Mountain. I've driven up the mountain more times than I've hiked it, but one time my husband and I hiked from bottom to top along with my good friend Sharon.

On our visits, as we near the top of the mountain, we often anticipate seeing a marvelous view of more mountains, scattered homes, and winding roads. However, many times our view ends up being clouded with a dense fog. The fog restricts our view, and causes the air to feel chilly and damp. After journeying to the mountain's peak, we would gather for a picnic with family and friends, and build a fire perfect for roasting hot dogs and marshmallows. The fire would warm us as we sat in the cloud, trying to enjoy the view.

A cloud that hides the view for just one day is bearable, especially if you're enjoying the time with your family and friends. However, those clouds that hover day after day or week after week can mess with my mind.

I've never been officially diagnosed with Seasonal Affective Disorder, but I've learned that I need sunshine to thrive. It boosts my mood and gives me energy. On days when I type during a string of cloudy days, I have a blinding "happy lamp" shining in my eyes. One winter I purchased this lamp to help imitate the sun on dreary days. The lamp doesn't warm me like the sunshine would, but somehow its brightness tricks my brain into thinking the sun is shining, and my mood becomes a little lighter.

I'm using this lamp right now as I write, because for more than two weeks we've only had a couple of glimpses of blue skies here in the Washington, D.C. area. It's May now—shouldn't it feel like summertime? I want to be warmed by the sun. I want to feel energized when I walk outside!

Instead, the clouds hang over my head like a depression. That's how disappointment has felt in my life, like nonstop clouds when I simply desire sunshine. One of those seasons of disappointment hovered over me as a young adult.

Growing Up

As I remember it, my childhood was almost idyllic. My life was stable, secure, overall very happy. I had two parents who loved each other (and still do), who rarely fought in front of their kids, and who did their best to teach their children to love God. My dad worked hard outside the home, and my mom was a full-time wife and mom. Throughout my childhood and teen years, our home was a safe place for my friends, my siblings, and me. I didn't have financial worries, plus my parents taught us how to understand and manage money at a young age. Through my school years I spent nearly equal thirds of my training in a Christian school, home school, and public school. I learned to play a couple of instruments and participated on a couple of sports teams. I read a lot of books and enjoyed being creative. My childhood wasn't perfect, but it was really good.

I suspect that all those good things probably made my transition to adulthood a little harder. Having never worried about money, it was challenging when I moved out on my own and had to pay for things like food and water and electricity. Having observed my parents' healthy marriage, I had a very hard time in my twenties as I watched my friends' Christian marriages crumble. Maybe I was a little sheltered as a child—but my world was secure.

As my high school graduation neared, I didn't want to attend college. My dreams consisted of being a wife and a mom, and maybe a writer, or maybe a missionary, but I didn't need a degree for any of those things! That's when I went away to Panama for five months of missionary school.

I returned home to my parents and siblings, changed from those months away, struggling to transition back to what was probably an above-average American lifestyle after living in a poorer country. Emotionally I struggled because I felt so purposeless. Proverbs 29:18 (KJV) says, "Where there is no vision, the people perish." I had no idea what to do with my life, and I felt pretty worthless. I was 19 years old, having spent my teen years in a Christian culture that told me I could be a world changer, and I was completely lost.

What would I do with my life? Yes, I had vague ideas of what I wanted to do with my adult life, but how would I get there?

My parents told me to start by getting a job. So I did what we did before the internet was used for such things: I opened up the newspaper and searched the "now hiring" ads.

A job opening at a photography store caught my eye. I knew where this photography store was within our local mall, so I stopped by to pick up an application. I filled out the paper application for this seasonal job and returned it to the store. I do not recall whether I had a formal interview, but I do recall being offered the job—as the mall Easter Bunny. (I still wonder if they hired me just because my last name then was Hopper. What a perfect name for a bunny.)

I needed a job and felt grateful that this one seemed easy and provided plenty of hours, so I accepted. I learned the ropes of my new job quickly. Arrive at the photography store wearing comfy clothes, put on the Easter Bunny costume in the back room, walk out to the center of the mall, wave at mall walkers and shoppers, sit in the large carrot-shaped chair, hold children on my lap while the photographer takes a photo. Sounds easy and fun, right?

Hour after hour, day after day, for several weeks, I sat on that carrot chair. I watched people roam the mall, and I made small talk with anyone who stopped by to see the Easter Bunny. I experienced some awkward moments, like when a teenage couple I had gone to high school with came to get their photo taken sitting on the Easter Bunny's lap.

A woman handed me her newborn baby for a photo, and the infant nearly slipped out of my huge gloved rabbit paws. The customer was angry that the Easter Bunny almost dropped her child, but I was annoyed that someone would hand the Easter Bunny such a tiny baby. Another day someone brought a preschool class to get their photo made, and the teacher put the rowdiest child on my lap for me to restrain.

The hardest part of my first real job was how I felt behind my mask. I was overwhelmed with feelings of disappointment with myself and my circumstances, battling feelings of depression every day. Customers didn't know it, but at times I was crying behind my mask.

You see, I thought I was supposed to launch forth into something exciting when I finished high school. Not interested in a career that required a college degree, I ran off to the mission field. It was exciting, but it was hard. It was really hard. When I came home, I had no idea how to cope or what to do with myself.

I felt disappointed with my life, and I felt disappointed with myself. This disappointment hovered over me like a cloud, leaving me feeling depressed, hopeless, and worthless, as a young woman whose life was still before her.

Around that time, I heard God's whisper in the first prophetic word anyone had ever spoken to me. "God is pleased with you, Betsy." I cried when the person praying for me said those words. How could God be pleased with me?

For weeks, I hid behind that Easter Bunny mask with tears in my eyes, because I didn't know who I was or where I was going in life. Disappointment hovered over me, giving me a chronic stomachache and many tears.

To this day, when I walk through a mall near Easter time and see a big rabbit in a carrot chair awaiting photos with families, I cringe as I remember that season. Thankfully, our focus isn't on the Easter Bunny. As we celebrate the resurrection of Jesus, encounters with His cross impact me even more.

The Cross

It's at the cross where Jesus said, "My God, my God, why have you forsaken Me?" (Matthew 27:46)

I might have felt like God had forgotten about little 19-year-old me weeping behind her mask, my self-pity might have made me feel forsaken by God, but I was never forgotten by Him. He's the one who whispered, "I am pleased with you, Betsy." Why? Because He created me, because He's my loving Father who liked me just because I was His, not because of what I was doing or not doing with my life.

In that moment on that first Good Friday thousands of years ago, Jesus, who had never sinned or done anything to deserve the wrath of God, died upon a cross for our behalf. His Father turned away because of the load of sin that Jesus carried. In that moment, Jesus said, "Why have you forsaken me?"

Despite my memories of that spring when disappointment and depression hovered over me, this season we call spring holds two magnificent things: Resurrection Sunday (which many call Easter) is the day when we remember not just Jesus' death, but His resurrection. He overpowered death, came back to life, was reunited with His Father, and forever He is there as our Savior and Friend. Resurrection Sunday also reminds me of that cloud of disappointment being lifted.

CHAPTER 9

DISAPPOINTMENT

Come, Thou fount of every blessing,
Tune my heart to sing Thy grace,
Streams of mercy, never ceasing,
Call for songs of loudest praise.

Robert Robinson, hymnwriter

Have you ever accidentally hit a deer, or any other large animal, with your car? It's stressful. I've heard tales of people hitting a bear or a moose or a cow. Those accidents sound more traumatic, although I suppose it could make a good story to tell later. Considering that I've lived most of my life in the eastern United States (which is certainly deer country), these accidents with deer in the road happen easily and abruptly.

I already described the type of disappointment that sneaks in and hovers over us like a suffocating cloud. However, sometimes disappointment is more shocking, hitting us hard, like when we're driving down a dark country road and we hit a deer at full speed. I've experienced this more than once, and each time it happened in an instant, with the collision bringing forth all sorts of emotions: fear, anxiety, anger, and pity for that wild animal we just hit. The impact is startling for those in the car, sometimes even crippling to the vehicle.

One summer, my husband and I drove home from a weekend away at my grandparents' mountain home. We expected to reach our apartment well past midnight, and my husband was alert and driving while I slept in the passenger's seat. While driving full speed on the interstate, Mike saw a deer standing in the road and as he safely swerved, I awoke. We felt the impact as the deer collided with the car. We were grateful that the impact happened on the front side of the car, between the driver's door and the headlight. We thanked God that our vehicle was minimally damaged, and we continued traveling toward our home.

I felt shaken up, unable to sleep again, and remembered a certain late night drive when I was a senior in high school. My two best friends and I were driving home from visiting friends in a neighboring town late one night. As I drove along the two-lane road through the mountains of West Virginia, I remember looking ahead at something on the far side of the street.

"Is that a deer?" I asked my passengers. Before anyone could answer, while my eyes were on the deer in the opposite lane, I hit the deer that was standing in my own lane. The poor deer didn't survive, and we three frantic teenage girls didn't know what to do. Cell phones were a recent invention, and I happened to have one. My archaic cell phone was big and clunky, and it only worked when plugged into the car's cigarette lighter, but we couldn't get any phone reception in the mountains that night anyway. We drove a little further until we found a house with lights on, where we knocked on the door and timidly asked to use their home phone to call our parents so someone could rescue us.

Many years later, I felt a similar unexpected impact on my emotions not long after my husband and I realized that pregnancy wasn't coming as easily as we had hoped. Disappointment and grief clouded my heart. This was one of my greatest dreams, and it felt impossible to achieve due to unexplained infertility. Month after month we hoped for a baby, and each month felt the grief, the lack, and the intense heartbreak. Close friends and family passed me by, birthing baby after baby.

One winter I had my eye on a newly married friend, wondering if she would become pregnant before me. Mentally I prepared myself that she could announce a pregnancy at any time. As we approached Christmas, I wasn't expecting an announcement from her. In fact, I wasn't expecting an announcement from anyone close to me. I felt like I could finally handle the holiday without baby grief!

Then, suddenly like the impact from the deer standing in my lane while my eyes were focused on the animal across the street, another close friend told me she was expecting another baby.

Didn't she already have a baby THIS YEAR? I vented my feelings toward my God, who has always listened to me patiently. *And now she's having another? Do you know that I've been trying to get pregnant for half a decade, God, and she gets two babies a year apart? Why, God, why?* The emotions of a woman grieving from barrenness are powerful.

Sing!

"Sing, barren woman! Shout for joy!" Of all the things a person might want to do in a barren place, singing as described in Isaiah 54:1 is probably not one of them. We might want to hide, to wallow, to cry, or pull away from others, but do we want to sing joyfully?

That baby announcement came while we were traveling to visit family, and it weighed on my mind as we drove along the familiar highways. I took a turn at the wheel while my husband rested in the passenger's seat. I plugged in my earphones and tried to cheer myself up as I drove.

I listened to the audio Bible. I still felt blue. I turned on Christian worship music. Yet I still felt so miserable, lost in my grief. I realized that the best thing I could do was to open my mouth and sing. I needed to focus on God by using the very air in my lungs and the energy in my body. In spite of my bad mood, I began to sing songs of worship to God, and the sadness lifted. It didn't go away completely, and I still had to work through my grief in days and weeks to come, but singing shifted my perspective and shifted my mood that day. I discovered the gift of singing through my barrenness.

I'm convinced that something happens when we saturate ourselves in joyful music, move our bodies a little, and use our breath to sing out loud. I encourage you to take a moment to sing a hymn, such as, "Come, Thou fount of every blessing, tune my heart to sing Thy grace." Let those words sink in.

While you take a shower or drive to work, sing your prayers to

God, make up new songs as you go, or simply sing to God that He is so good. If you can play a guitar or piano or ukulele, then sing along with your instrument, but regardless of what you do, just sing! It seems that singing just for the sake of singing is a lost art. In my childhood and teen years, we would often sing in the car just for fun. These days, playing music digitally is so quick and easy that we often find ourselves listening more than singing. But I believe that singing out loud is beneficial!

When I'm singing out loud, I'm listening to the words and I'm also contemplating them. Do I believe these words I'm singing? That in Christ alone my hope is found? That whatever happens, I can choose to say that it is well with my soul? That whatever He gives or takes away, I will still praise Him?

Words hold power. We can meditate on the rich theology found through singing old hymns. Faith comes from hearing the Word of God. (Romans 10:17) Singing the truth of God's Word back to Him forces me to think about it and it allows my faith to arise. Yes, I can sing a song because I believe it, and while I'm singing, the message is being reinforced into my mind and heart.

When my soul was in the most barren of seasons and I was longing for a child, you might have seen me on a Sunday morning at church, singing to my Heavenly Father with desperation. Well, you might not have noticed my anguish, since I would usually bow my head or allow my hair fall over my face to hide my tears. On brighter days I would sing those faith-filled songs in church as a declaration that I believed that all of God's promises are yes and amen and that Jesus is my hope and that He's the King of my heart.

These days, with my arms full, I don't feel the same desperation, but I still sing these words of truth and proclaim God's faithfulness over other areas of my life. Because I know the ache of the barren woman so well, when I see a woman with an unfulfilled longing for children pouring her heart out in worship, I find it to be beautiful. I have watched these women in worship services, knowing that their hearts are deeply longing for God to change their circumstances. Knowing some of these women personally, I can also attest to the trust they have in their Heavenly Father. As they sing, the tension is reflected on their faces: longing for something different but trusting God's sovereignty.

Wrestling Through It

I continued to wrestle with my emotions that week, celebrating Christmas on the outside and reeling with emotion on the inside. Mike, who is like my rock of support, heard me say several times throughout the holidays that I was simply trying to make it through each day.

I realized that my pregnant friend wasn't trying to hurt me by making her own joyful announcement. In fact, she was quite sensitive to my feelings. She was just living her life, which included having babies. And I was simply living my life, which meant trying to have a baby, but not succeeding.

During the week of festivities, the Lord allowed me to put my finger on the feeling that overwhelmed me: disappointment.

At that point, we had experienced about 70 cycles of trying to get pregnant, with no success, even with surgery and medication that were supposed to help. I had written a book and started a blog about having hope during infertility—because I was clinging to a God-given hope that He is able. Despite my faith and hope, I kept feeling the impact of disappointment over and over again.

Christmas and that surprise baby announcement came just before my birthday and New Year's Day. As the New Year began, I contemplated the past year's milestones and unfulfilled dreams. Unfortunately, many years I wrap up the year focused on what didn't happen instead of rejoicing in all the good that did happen! For years I had been longing for something at Christmas that couldn't be gift wrapped. During my twenties I wished for a husband, and after getting married, I started hoping for a baby. In my mind, the holiday season was often associated with disappointment.

A barren womb wasn't the only struggle Mike and I faced during those years. Although I am grateful to have a kind, caring, God-loving husband, his career transition left him without work longer than we anticipated. Our finances were much tighter than we preferred. I was childless and working full time outside of the home although I dreamed about being a full-time mom.

As I've struggled with feelings of emptiness in various areas of life, I have wondered if unfulfilled dreams and disappointment are going to define me forever.

Not long after that Christmas when that baby announcement hit me hard, the Washington, D.C. area where we lived was hit with a major snow storm. I spent several extra days at home with my husband, in our warm basement apartment, grateful that our electricity stayed on through the storm. I baked, I rested, I organized, and I wrote. Ultimately, I enjoyed the break from our normal busy lives. During those years of working long hours, I often dreamed of simply being at home.

God's blessings were in that snowstorm that kept us home together for several days. God gave me the opportunity to stay at home for days on end, to just "be" in our home. God gave me a gift by answering a small desire of my heart, and He reminded me to be grateful for the little joys—even the joy of not having to go to work on a Monday! I enjoyed working on projects in the warmth of our home while watching the snow from our window.

My feelings were conflicted due to my frustration over the big things (fertility and finances) and delight from the little things (snow days and small blessings). I began to consider how I could rejoice in all things, in both the big discouragements as well as the little delights.

When disappointment clouded all hope and joy, the devil whispered: *Betsy, your life is a disappointment. You're stuck in your job. Marketing your first book has been more work than you ever imagined. You'll never be a homeowner. And do you really think you'll still get pregnant? Medical tests prove that your fertility is declining.*

How about you? What disappointment is jumping into your path in the darkness of night? What disappointment is hovering over your head trying to suffocate you? Maybe you're disappointed by an attempted achievement: you didn't pass your audition into that musical group, your writing was rejected by a publisher again, or you can't seem to find a decent job.

Disappointments surround our families: maybe your family has let you down, or someone has abused you. Maybe you dream of having your own family, but marriage or motherhood seem to be impossible. Maybe you have a spouse and children, but you feel miserable inside because things have not turned out like you hope.

Proverbs 14:10 says, "Each heart knows its own bitterness, and no one else can share its joy." Each and every one of us holds some pain, difficulty, or discouragement in our heart that nobody else can fully understand. However, God does truly know and understand what's going on.

Even when our circumstances seem to be rotten, we have a choice to make. Is disappointment going to characterize my life?

On a cloudy winter day, while trekking through a barren forest and contemplating my barren womb and overwhelming grief, I sensed the Holy Spirit telling me that I do not have to be defined by disappointment. He reminded me that I can instead rest in the knowledge that God has appointed Himself over me and my circumstances. Although the trees were not in bloom and the forest wasn't seemingly full of life, there was peace and beauty in that barren place. That day I chose to believe that I don't have to be defined by disappointment, even in my most barren of places, I can walk with my Creator in peace and beauty.

If the enemy of my soul is trying to bog me down with feelings of disappointment, I know that he is going directly against what God intends. Which makes me wonder: what is the opposite of disappointment, anyway?

That January, I wondered which word would define my year. After asking God to give me a word for the year ahead, I pondered for a while, then narrowed it down to two hyphenated words: God-appointment.

God-appointments

I believe that God-appointments are greater than my disappointments, even if they're a tiny hope fulfilled within a greater forgotten dream. As I described at the beginning of this book, I wasn't able to travel into Sudan with my dad years ago when I became sick. My unexpected week in Kenya ultimately fulfilled a forgotten hope. Surely it was a divine appointment.

The word appointment can refer to a meeting at a specific time, or someone being appointed for a certain role. God-appointments include those divine appointments when God surprises us with just the right thing at just the right time.

God-appointments are when we remember that He has appointed Himself over us and over our circumstances. He knows what He's doing, His timing is right, and His plans are good. Sometimes we can't understand His divine timing; other times we can't stop thanking Him for it.

One sunny spring day as I was beginning to write this book, I met a friend for coffee. We sat outside talking and sipping our drinks, watching the clouds roll in. As the rain drops began to fall, we headed toward our cars, and I began driving down the busy four-lane road toward my home near Washington, D.C. After stopping for a stoplight, only one car was in the stretch of road ahead of me. I watched as a very tall tree to the right of the road swayed in the wind then began falling into the street. I instinctively pushed the brake with my foot, watching the other car also come to a stop as this tree fell across all four lanes of traffic directly in front of us. It was remarkable that no cars passed through at that moment. I felt such gratitude to God that He had allowed me to leave at the perfect time, then to wait at a crosswalk for ambling pedestrians to cross in just the right amount of time. Because His timing was so exact, the tree did not injure me or damage my car, nor did it hit anyone else. I knew that moment was a God-appointment.

God protects both you and me in countless situations. Sometimes we are aware of it, sometimes we are oblivious. God has also appointed you and me to live right now in this time and place. No matter how difficult this year has been for us, He intended us to live here and now. He's the one writing your life story and mine. My story hasn't gone according to my plan, but His appointment matters the most.

Our disappointments can be used by God to redirect our lives and draw us toward Himself. Rejoicing in God-appointments instead of focusing on disappointments will only make our lives more enjoyable. I believe that this is a key to thriving instead of surviving. This applies to the big things and the small ones. Even this morning, I wanted to be writing, but I needed to take care of some mundane household chores first. I began singing "God is so good" while I worked. The minor disappointment I felt turned into gladness, and not long after, I found time to sit down and focus on writing. Focusing on God's goodness instead of our disappointment will always benefit us.

If I shouldn't dwell on my feelings of disappointment in the middle of disappointing circumstances, what am I to focus on? If God's goodness and mercy are following me through all the days of my life as mentioned in Psalm 23, I simply need to look for His goodness, thank Him for it, and talk about it! I'm polishing up this manuscript for publication in 2020, feeling the effects of the worldwide pandemic, feeling sad for the pain felt all across America. The pandemic, economic struggles, racial tension, and natural disasters are just a few things hurting people I know.

The memes and jokes I see online demonstrate that many people feel like this year is a big disappointment. Some wonderful things have happened in my personal life this year, but at the same time, it has been a lonely year. Do I focus on my loneliness, or do I focus on the good? God's goodness is here, in the land of the living. God's goodness is here, in 2020. I choose to make the declaration that God is so good as I thank Him for all the good things I can think of, no matter how small.

It might take a lifetime to learn how to choose joy over sorrow or negativity, but I want to focus on God-appointments instead of letdowns. Let's learn to appreciate the "wave" that brings us closer to the Rock of Ages.

In the big picture of our lives, God knows what He's doing. He's going to work everything together for our good. Romans 8:28 says,

"And we know that in all things God works for the good of those who love him, who have been called according to his purpose."

It's like baking cookies. The individual ingredients might taste gross. Plain flour. A mouthful of salt or baking soda. But when everything is mixed together, it creates something very good! We can look at the ingredients of our life circumstances and wonder, "Hey God, exactly how are you working this out for my good?" However, we must trust that He knows what He's doing. He's making a delicious cookie out of flour and salt and sugar and eggs. He's going to put those things together and put them into the fire. Individual ingredients might seem yucky, but ultimately, something good is being formed.

If you're facing trials or struggling with disappointment because things aren't going the way you expected, trust God's call on your life and have hope, knowing that He is working it out for good. Taking note of God's surprises and His divine appointments will shift our perspective.

CHAPTER 10

HOPE AND FAITH

**Faith is the confidence
that what we hope for
will actually happen;
it gives us assurance about
things we cannot see.**

Hebrews 11:1 (NLT)

Get Your Hopes Up

One afternoon I informed the children I was babysitting that their mother was coming home from work early so that she could go to a hair appointment. "Ooh, I want to go with her!" one child exclaimed, and another said, "I'm going to ask her if I can go too!"

Knowing that they want to spend time with their mom and go places with her, but realizing that she might not want to take her little ones to her hair appointment, I matter-of-factly warned the kids: "You may ask your mom, but she will probably tell you no."

"You're getting our hopes down!" one of the children replied.

I smiled at her use of words, since people normally talk about getting their hopes up. Yet that idea stuck with me, because I know what it's like to get my hopes down.

Building our faith involves getting our hopes up even when it hurts. Anyone who has attempted to live a life of faith and hope in God has probably experienced the tension of wanting to believe that God will act in a certain way while wrestling with the nagging fear that asks, "Well, what if He doesn't?" Something I've learned while waiting for God to bring certain things to pass is that often He's much slower than we expect, and His plans are different. How do we trust in His timing as we grow in faith?

A passage of Scripture that has encouraged me and many others as we await God's timing is Habakkuk 2:3 (The Living Bible): "But these things I plan won't happen right away. Slowly, steadily, surely, the time approaches when the vision will be fulfilled. If it seems slow, do not despair, for these things will surely come to pass. Just be patient! They will not be overdue a single day!"

I loved that translation of this verse when I was a teenager, and I laugh today wondering what it was that I felt so desperate for back then. I had what I needed at that time—a good family, parents who cared for my needs, an education, and hope for the future.

Maybe I was caught up in the idea of romance and wondered if I would ever find my special someone? Was that the vision I was hoping would come to pass? Eventually I met and married my husband and we were met with new challenges. Infertility brought us an opportunity to hope, to feel disappointment, and to hope again.

Don't Mislead Me

While cleaning out a closet one day years before I became pregnant, I opened a box to find maternity clothes waiting patiently for me to wear. Deep in our closets sat bags of baby clothes and baby girl crib bedding that I hoped to use someday. Several plastic tubs of secondhand baby items waited for us in the attic at my parents' house. These items remind me of the hope that I held onto, even when hoping seemed crazy.

Around the time that I rediscovered my box of maternity clothes, I was reading through Ezekiel, and a verse popped out at me. These words were spoken from the Lord to His people. "None of my words will be delayed any longer; whatever I say will be fulfilled, declares the Sovereign Lord," I read in Ezekiel 12:28.

I underlined it. For several days I thought about it.

Do you want to know how I felt about it?

I felt like the Shunammite woman in 2 Kings 4. She was kind and hospitable to Elisha, the prophet. She welcomed him, fed him meals, and even made up a guest room in her home for him to use when he was in her town. This woman was married, but had no children. One day the prophet, Elisha, said to his servant, "What can we do for her?" He replied, "Well, she doesn't have a son and her husband is old." Elisha called the woman in and said to her, "About this time next year, you will hold a son in your arms."

She replied, "No, don't mislead me!"

I imagine the emotions she is feeling: I want to have hope! But this hurts! This is my greatest desire, my unfulfilled dream, a tender place in my heart that just hurts! Don't tell me that it will happen. Can't you see that it hasn't happened after all this time!?

Despite her reaction, 2 Kings 4:17 says, "But the woman became pregnant, and the next year about that same time she gave birth to a son, just as Elisha had told her."

Even when a heartfelt response to a word from God is not that of faith, even when it is full of pain and doubt, God is still able to perform a miracle.

How does this apply to us? For those experiencing infertility, here are a few things to consider. The Bible doesn't promise that everyone will have the family they desire. However, the Bible does tell a lot of stories about infertility, and in the Bible, every woman who asked God for a baby eventually had a baby. As we prayed and walked with God, my husband and I sensed that God had children for us. Eventually, God answered our prayers and brought us children. At the same time, I have walked alongside friends entering their 40s and 50s whose prayers for a family have not been answered the same way. The reality is that sometimes we just don't understand why God doesn't answer our prayers in the way we know is possible. I continue to grapple with this mystery, allowing my questions to draw me closer to God.

We can all choose to have hope that God is able—even when our given situation seems impossible. Even if we feel more like the Shunammite woman than we would prefer.

Sometimes we forget about the rest of the Shunammite woman's story. She gave birth to her long-awaited, prophesied, miracle baby.

Several years later, her son had a headache and he died. Her faith had been strengthened, now it was mighty! She laid the child in bed and went directly to Elisha the prophet who had prophesied this child's birth. When Elisha came to the family's home, the power of God brought the child back to life. The story is recorded in 2 Kings 4.

God's power demonstrates that He can truly do anything. We need to remind ourselves: "Get your hopes up! He can do anything!" Yet, we tend to get our hopes down because we've known disappointment. We've asked God for something and He hasn't answered the way we desired. People who believed God would heal them of cancer died without being healed. Parents whose children have died have asked God to revive them, to bring them back to life, and it has not happened. The list goes on.

I remind myself that God can do anything, but ultimately my hope is not in what He can do—my hope is in Him. He is God. He is good. He is wise. He is the great I am.

Faith

Hebrews 11:1 says, "Now faith is confidence in what we hope for and assurance about what we do not see." This Scripture continually speaks to me, since I'm always in the process of believing that things I hope for will happen, even with disappointments along the way. I am challenged when I remember that the book of Hebrews points out that many heroes of our faith died while still waiting for their promise from God to come to pass. That's what faith is—believing with all our hearts that God will do it, believing that with Him all things are possible, and holding onto that belief even until the grave.

Faith involves waiting for God to answer even though we know it's a possibility that He will not answer us the way we think that He will. How are we to keep living by faith when our prayers are not answered? Maybe they will be answered as we desire, but when we don't know that for sure, how do we continue to trust?

When our circumstances of waiting, barrenness, and disappointment confuse us, a statement Jesus made to his followers rings true: "You do not realize now what I am doing, but later you will understand." (John 13:7) God's ways don't have to make sense to us right now.

My greatest opportunity to grow in faith while writing this book was in my desire to have children. After years of being unable to conceive, I learned to exercise my faith to strengthen it. Looking back throughout history as well as hearing stories of modern day miracles helped my faith to grow.

For example, I think of the many people in the Bible who had a tough journey through infertility before their miracle babies were born. Abraham and Sarah were promised offspring, but baby Isaac didn't come along for many decades.

Was Isaac then guaranteed a wonderful life? He married Rebekah when he was 40—and that marriage was without a doubt a divine appointment (see Genesis 24). However, it took them 20 years to become pregnant! The Bible simply says that Isaac prayed; however, I wonder if they questioned God during their long wait. Did they wonder what was wrong with them, or did Isaac's own birth story remind them that God is able to bring forth a miraculous pregnancy? In hindsight, we can see that God had a good plan, and He gave Isaac and Rebekah twins.

Jacob, one of those twins, fathered the sons who became the leaders of the twelve tribes of Israel, but not without difficulty. He had two wives, which was not unusual for that day. He was also given a maidservant by each wife, a woman with whom to bear more children. Of the four women, his favorite wife, Rachel, was unable to become pregnant for several years. Yet she did eventually have babies, and one of those sons was Joseph, who led nations through a tough time of famine. His God-given wisdom in God's right timing kept thousands of people alive during years when the earth was barren.

There are many other references to infertility in the Bible, but one of my favorite Bible stories is that of Elizabeth and Zechariah. He was a priest; she was his wife. They were an upstanding, God-loving couple. They were old and everyone knew they were barren. Obviously they had no children in a time and place where producing offspring was culturally expected.

Just before Jesus was conceived in Mary by the Holy Spirit, the Creator of life allowed this older couple to become pregnant with John. When Elizabeth discovered she was pregnant she said in Luke 1:25: "The Lord has done this for me… He has shown His favor and taken away my disgrace among the people."

The angel Gabriel came to Mary to let her know she would be the mother of the Messiah. She asked him how that could happen since she was a virgin.

Gabriel told her that "even Elizabeth your relative is going to have a child in her old age, and she who was said to be unable to conceive is in her sixth month. For no word from God will ever fail." I prefer the 1984 printing of the NIV version that calls Elizabeth "old and barren," and instead of "no word from God will ever fail," that particular translation declares, "Nothing is impossible with God."

I wrote this chapter after six years of trying to have a baby. I clung to that very Scripture, remembering that when it comes to women getting pregnant, nothing is impossible with God. No matter what area of your life is past its peak and barren, I want to remind you that nothing is impossible with God. Let's get our hopes up, believing that God is able to answer our prayers even after we stop praying them.

CHAPTER 11

OFFENDED BY GOD

...blessed is he who is not offended because of Me.

Matthew 11:6 (NKJV)

Have you ever felt offended toward God, perhaps feeling upset or disgruntled because of the way that He does things? When John the Baptist was out and about preaching and preparing the way for Jesus' ministry, he was doing what he was called by God to do. His life was different than many, beginning with a unique prophecy about his birth to an older, childless couple. As an adult, he traveled in the wilderness and ate locusts and wild honey. He preached and prepared the way for Jesus. However, he was still thrown into jail by Herod, the ruler of their day. Even after a miraculous birth and divine calling, he still found himself imprisoned.

From his jail cell, he heard about Jesus' ministry—people were being healed, lives were being changed, and great things were happening! As he sat in his jail cell, he began wondering what was going on.

Luke 7:18-19 says: "John's disciples told him about all these things. Calling two of them, he sent them to the Lord to ask, 'Are you the one who is to come, or should we expect someone else?'"

In verses 22-23, Jesus replied, "Go back and report to John what you have seen and heard: The blind receive sight, the lame walk, those who have leprosy are cleansed, the deaf hear, the dead are raised, and the good news is proclaimed to the poor. Blessed is anyone who does not stumble on account of me."

Matthew 11 also recounts this story. Verse 6 (NKJV) says, "And blessed is he who is not offended because of Me."

"Not offended because of me." Jesus' words echo in my mind.

While growing older and waiting for my own miracle baby, experiencing failed attempts at getting pregnant, I battled ongoing painful disappointments that tempted me to feel offended at God. I often wondered why God would take so long to answer good and simple prayers.

I've had this conversation with many women who desire marriage, and with many married women who desire to have children. We're not asking for extravagant things; we are asking God for a husband or children. For years, I was single and asking God for a husband, and then for the first eight years of our married life, we asked God to bless us with children.

Maybe you're asking God for financial provision and you're still struggling. You might need breakthrough in a relationship or you're asking God for healing. You feel like you're knocking on Heaven's door, crying out for Him to change things, wondering if He ever will.

Maybe you're feeling stuck in a rut at your job, and you're asking God for something new. Maybe you're trying to find work, submitting countless applications for jobs without any doors of opportunity being opened.

Whatever it is that you're hoping God will do in your life, if you're not seeing Him answer, you might be starting to feel offended by God's way of doing things.

John heard about how Jesus was setting people free and healing them. Meanwhile, he was staring at the wall of a jail cell, likely with shackles on his hands and feet. Couldn't Jesus miraculously release John from prison? We know that Jesus could only act upon His Father's will (John 5:19). We don't always understand why God doesn't change our circumstances when it's within His power to do so.

Jesus' message to John was simple. He told John to not be offended by the way He was doing things. We can all learn from Jesus' words: "Do not be offended by me."

John heard stories of all the miracles that Jesus is performing: the blind can see again, the crippled people are walking and jumping, people with the incurable disease of leprosy are healed, and the list goes on. I imagine that John is thinking, "If Jesus can help them, why doesn't He help me?"

Jesus' response to John was essentially this: "Yes, I'm out here doing all these miracles while you're in there feeling disappointed, but don't allow feelings of offense to cause you to fall away from trusting me."

I've been over here thinking, *Hey God, I feel disappointed by my life's circumstances.*

God whispers to my heart, "Do not be offended by the way I orchestrate things." In this journey of learning to trust God through all circumstances and seasons of my life, I want to trust Him through my deepest disappointments.

John was not released from prison. Instead, he was killed there. Were those the last words John ever heard from Jesus? What was the last word God whispered to you?

How long was John in prison from the time he heard Jesus' message until he died? When he knew that Jesus was setting everyone free but he was stuck in a jail cell, did Jesus' words echo in his mind repeatedly? I imagine John's thoughts could have gone like this:

Hey Jesus, you're doing miracles, can't you get me out of here?

"Do not be offended by Me."

I'm your cousin—why are you leaving me in jail?

"Do not be offended by Me."

I was born to my parents late in life because You had a special purpose for my life! Is this really Your plan for me to be in jail right now or to die so young?

"Do not be offended by Me."

In my own journey of disappointment, I hear God saying the same thing when I complain to Him.

But God, can't you give BOTH of us babies? Why just her?

"Do not be offended by Me."

God, unemployment has lasted too long, and our finances have been strained too long.

"Do not be offended by Me."

Hey God, this year is not going like I had hoped or expected.

"Do not be offended by Me."

What if God never says yes to your desperate prayers or mine? I believe that He is a God of miracles, and He can do anything. I also believe that He's sovereign, and He is going to work everything out for His own glory and my good, even if I don't understand it during my lifetime.

I choose to believe that God is good and that He is good toward me even if my prayers aren't answered the way I would like them to be answered. John the Baptist was killed even after his parents waited a lifetime for him to be born and even though God called Him for a special purpose. His story didn't end like you or I might have thought that it should. Yet the circumstances do not change God's goodness.

Can I choose to not be offended by the way God does things? Can I still walk through life with faith instead of fear? Will I choose to not be offended by Him while at the same time continuing to believe?

I believe that offense is closely tied to control. We often feel offended by other people because they're not doing things the way we want them to. I cannot control that person's actions, so instead I'm offended by them. The reason I could be offended toward God is because He's not doing things the way I think He should.

I imagine John would have been thinking something like this: "I'm in jail, about to die. Letting me live would be better than this!" Yet Jesus said, "Do not be offended by me."

While writing this book I could say, "God, I'd like better financial provision for our family. God, I'd like to be done having kids by now instead of still trying to get started." Instead, I should say, "I trust You."

In my deepest pain, as I look to God and wonder why He hasn't answered as I hoped, I can trust His goodness and His decision. I hear Him whisper, "Do not be offended by me." Will I choose to be unoffended by the way that God chooses to orchestrate my life?

If Not

We all have "if not" or "what if" questions. What if it doesn't happen? What if my disappointments never resolves with a happy ending? What if the barren woman never becomes a mom? What if people who are offended by me never speak to me again? What if I struggle financially for the rest of my life? What if God never answers these prayers we're praying?

God didn't rescue John from prison. I've known many God-loving people who asked Him for healing from cancer, yet they died at a younger age than we would have liked. While attending the funeral of one of those people, I heard a sermon that reflected on John, in prison. In his final days, was John reminding himself of the words he had spoken in John 3:30 (NKJV): "He [Jesus] must increase, but I must decrease."

How can we live our lives so that God's glory increases, even if things don't go like we want them to?

Even though every woman we read about in the Bible who asked God for a baby eventually had a baby, I know many women today who have prayed the same thing, yet have grown older without giving birth. It causes me to wrestle with the questions, "What if God doesn't answer my prayers? What if circumstances never change?"

I've been pondering the story of Shadrach, Meshach, and Abednego, a classic Bible story I learned as a child, about how King Nebuchadnezzar made a golden idol and required everyone to bow down to it. These three followers of God refused to bow.

When brought before the king, these men were warned that they must bow to the idol or be thrown into the fire.

"What God could rescue you from a fiery furnace?" the king asked them. They chose obedience to God. Knowing they would be thrown into the furnace, these three men told the king that they knew God could rescue them. And if not? They still chose faith over fear.

Popular Christian art reflects this passage in Daniel 3 with the words, "And if not, He is still good." When I studied this Bible passage, I realized that phrase was not actually in the Bible, then I read something that summarized the message so well.

Kelly Streiff, writer, speaker, and founder of the *Even If* podcast described this "and if not, He's still good" paraphrase perfectly in an Instagram post. In her podcast she digs deep into grief and articulates God's goodness throughout one of the greatest heartaches I can imagine—the loss of a child. Kelly shared the following words five months after her long-awaited daughter Imogen was stillborn:

And if not, He is still good.

These are the words we held onto while we were in the hospital waiting and laboring for Imogen to be born.

We fixed our EXPECTATION on what God was able to do:

He can resurrect and completely heal our baby girl! Our God will do it!

But we fixed our HEART on who God is even when he doesn't:

And if not, He is still good.

I've declared this in a lot of hopeless seasons in my life. I've carried the tension of confident expectation in what God can do and irrational trust even when He doesn't.

But never more than we did in those hours.

In the weeks after we came home, I turned to those words once again. I thumbed through the pages until I found Daniel chapter 3 and started reading the familiar story.

Only, these words weren't there. I pulled up another translation. And another. It didn't matter where I looked, they just weren't there.

While, certainly, they're still true, that's not the declaration they made. What they actually said was, "Even if he does not [deliver us from this fire], we will not serve your gods..." (Daniel 3:18 HCSB)

We will not worship anything else. We will not bow.

And this distinction makes all the difference. Because the quote we hand-letter on everything from postcards to coffee mugs [rightfully] honors who GOD IS when we don't get the outcome we want.

But this scripture declares who WE WILL BE when

everything falls apart.

So my declaration has changed to encompass both the steadfastness of God's goodness AND my response in disappointment and devastation.

It is precisely because I'm convinced that God is good, no matter the pain of my circumstance, that I can stand firm and declare, "I will not give in to anything else."

Because HE is still good, WE will not bow.

See, God's character was never really in question.

But ours is up for grabs.[1]

Since God's character is good, and His character is unchanging, then our response is the issue at hand. How will we respond to Him during the worst of circumstances?

God is always good, and I'm determined that we can always look for and find His goodness. It won't change. However, our attitudes and responses waver. As a follower of Christ, I want to be steadfast, knowing that He is always good and faithful. I want my attitude to always reflect trust in Him.

Like these three men in the book of Daniel, when my circumstances seem hopeless, I can say that God is able to do a miracle.

And if not? I still choose to believe that God is good toward me. When life doesn't go at all like we want it to? We can trust God. When we are disappointed? He's still good, so we can remain steadfast. We must dig into God's Word so that His truth stabilizes us.

Believe that God can do the impossible, no matter what your trial looks like. Maybe you're in a situation where you could be killed for your faith. Maybe you simply want to give birth to children and mother them. Maybe you're asking God for a spouse, and time seems to be passing you by. Perhaps you are battling cancer or another life-threatening illness and you need a miracle to keep living. It could be that you want to birth a dream, or to see changes in your circumstances. Whatever situation you are praying for, you can choose to stand in faith, remembering that even if God doesn't answer the way you hope, He is still good, and you can choose to not be offended by Him.

I want to trust God in every situation for the rest of my life. Let's follow the example of John, who was in jail making a choice to not be offended by Jesus. Like Shadrach, Meshach, and Abednego, we can walk into whatever situation awaits us trusting that "if not, He's still good."

CHAPTER 12

OFFENDED BY OTHERS

Make every effort to live in peace with everyone...

Hebrews 12:14

What about when other people offend me? I don't even know where to begin on this topic of Christians disappointing and offending each other because I wish we had no need to discuss it. I'd prefer that difficult circumstances were my only disappointment. However, there are people who disappoint, and when fellow Christians hurt us or let us down, we must dig through the mess in our hearts.

First, let's start with the simplest of suggestions. Let's try to not be offended by others. What if we were unoffendable? Could we choose to be quick to forgive and difficult to upset? When someone causes us to feel stressed, when their child hurts ours, when we think they've wronged our loved one, let's choose to not hold a grudge. Forgiving as soon as possible will help us nip offense in the bud. Unfortunately, offense is often more complicated than a one-time, simple mistake.

Offense toward other people is often messy. It's painful. Often it's the people closest to us whom we offend. Somehow our closest friends and family are able to offend us. Why? Maybe we feel offended when others won't listen and do things our way. We try to control other people, and when they don't cooperate, we feel offended. Offense can also be rooted in jealousy. For example, when someone else gets what I want, I could feel offended by both the recipient and the giver. I'm sure that there are other roots to offense as well.

I have seen blatant jealousy rise up between young siblings. For example, one child receives a gift of candy, and his sibling feels angry and upset because she didn't. Maybe the jealous child screams and cries, or says unkind things to let everyone know how she feels about the perceived unfairness of the situation. As an adult watching a child being unnecessarily upset about candy, it might seem silly. I know that we shouldn't let our emotions get out of control over something so unimportant.

However, I do the same. Maybe you do too? One day I was at a friend's house, sitting in one room while listening to her young daughters playing with dolls in another room. I could hear the youngest sister complaining to the older ones: "But I want a turn to be the mommy! You always get to be the mommy and I want to be the mommy!" I chuckled when I heard that, knowing that's how I felt as a woman experiencing infertility. When a woman struggles to have a baby and sees her friends or sisters "always getting to be the mommy," she is prone to that same jealousy.

We shouldn't let our emotions get out of control for things large or small. I have felt hurt and frustrated when an opportunity I have been striving for is handed to someone else. Should I scream and throw a temper tantrum like a child?

I remember a specific week when two people I knew were given opportunities as writers and speakers—opportunities that I had also sought but not received. It stung to watch others be chosen instead of me. While crying on my husband's shoulder, wanting to wallow in my hurt feelings, God reminded me of the Scripture I had just taught the little children in Sunday school, "I have hidden your word in my heart that I might not sin against you." (Psalm 119:11) I know that God's word clearly lists jealousy as sin in Galatians 5, just before it describes the fruit of the Spirit. Overcoming offense requires us to deal with the sin in our own hearts—including jealousy.

Regularly I must ask myself: Will I choose to be offended, or will I let the fruit of the Spirit grow in my life? Love, joy, peace, patience, kindness, goodness, faithfulness, gentleness, self-control—those are the characteristics I would rather build in my life instead of offense, control, and jealousy.

It's a hard lesson to learn, even as an adult, and especially for a first-born like me. In my childhood, I was used to being first: for the first two years of my life, I was the only child, and I was the first to learn to talk, the first to walk, the first to go to school, the first to drive, the first to move out of my parents' home. I learned that I got to go first because I was here first. Traditionally, in the workplace, if you have the most training, or the most authority, or if you've been there the longest, then you get paid the most. It's logical, right?

Choosing Love

Jesus throws off our logic when explaining how His kingdom works. In Matthew 20, Jesus tells the parable of the landowner who was looking for some workers. Early in the morning he hired some guys to work on his land. A few hours later, he hired some more workers, and hours later, he hired even more. He did this all day long, and at the end of the day, it was time to pay the workers. You'd think they would be paid fairly based on who showed up first and who worked the longest, right? Those hired last, who worked just a little bit, were paid the promised amount. Those who were hired first were shocked to discover that they didn't receive any more pay than the latecomers.

The landowner asks a question worded in two different ways across many versions of the Bible. One question is "are you envious because I am generous?" (Matthew 20:15 NIV) When I'm feeling jealous of someone else, if Jesus stepped into the room and asked me that question, I'd feel humbled, realizing that He's in charge, and He can demonstrate generosity however He pleases.

Many Bible versions word the same question with the landowner asking, "Is your eye evil because I am good?" (Matthew 20:15 NKJV) When I'm looking through eyes of jealousy, I'm choosing an evil way of seeing a situation. God is generous, and He is always good.

Even if my feelings are legitimately hurt, even if I can justifiably say I was wronged by someone, I still get to choose my response. The Bible clearly says I'm supposed to rejoice with those who rejoice—not only when I feel happy about it. If someone else is rejoicing because they've been given an opportunity that I want—I am supposed to rejoice with them! Or if you're in elementary school, and your sister is eating a piece of candy that you want, you're supposed to be happy that she's getting to enjoy your favorite candy. Is it easy? No. Nobody said following God and His way of doing things is easy. Yet living unoffended toward God and others is freeing!

Love and Peace

Jesus' two greatest commandments are that I love God with my whole being, and that I love my neighbor as myself (Matthew 22:36-40). As I navigate offense and reconciliation within my life, I remember that God's word says that love covers a multitude of sins, and the poetic words in Song of Solomon 2:4 (NKJV) echo in my ears, "His banner over me was love." God's banner over me is love. The banner I should carry over relationships past and present is love.

The New Testament refers to followers of Christ as being many members of one body. Together we make up the Body of Christ. When one part of the body suffers, others suffer as well. As the body of Christ we are designed to work together with those placed beside of us. It's not coincidental that we hurt when someone close to us hurts. I have experienced headaches that throb all the way down my back. I've felt abdominal pain radiate into my legs. Why can I feel pain in a completely different body part than the source of the pain? Because I am one body, made up of many parts, and when one part hurts deeply

I can feel it elsewhere.

When another person in this Body of Christ is suffering, especially one closely connected to me, I'm designed to feel it. We are designed to work together, to pursue peace, and to not let a bitter root grow.

What should we do when Christians let us down? Most of us have been very disappointed by another Christian, and I'm sad to say that some people have been disappointed by me.

Offense between people builds up a wall between them. When John was in prison, he knew that Jesus had the ability to set him free. John had heard the voice of God declaring Jesus His beloved as he baptized Jesus. Yet he also heard those last words echo in his ears: *Do not be offended by me.*

It's easy to be angry, closing ourselves off in offense, but God's banner over His children is love, and we've got to move toward reconciliation and love when there has been offense.

If I want to see the goodness of God in my life, I cannot be looking through the lens of offense. If I'm seeing God through eyes of offense, or if I'm looking at my brothers and sisters in Christ from a perspective of offense, I will not be able to focus on God's goodness. Sometimes it might take extra effort to let love cover offense. 1 Peter 4:8 says, "Above all, love each other deeply, because love covers over a multitude of sins." Let's look through lenses of love, not offense.

When I'm hurt and about to let those feelings of offense take over, I can remember the wisdom of John Piper that I mentioned previously in this book. Even in the little things, we can follow his advice: "Weep deeply over the life you hoped would be. Grieve the losses. Then wash your face. Trust God. And embrace the life you have."

Instead of indulging in feelings of jealousy or offense, I should cry for a moment, then lift my head and embrace the life that God has given me. Instead of letting a bitter root grow up into a vine of destruction, I must dig up that root of jealousy or offense and get rid of it. Hebrews 12:15 admonishes us to not let a bitter root grow up inside us, defiling us. What does that mean?

Digging Up Roots

When I was in college, I had two goals: to find a husband and to graduate as soon as possible. I didn't find my husband there, although I did find lifelong friends. I did manage to graduate in less than four years, but looking back, I can see that I was totally stressed out all the time and I should have slowed down. (Maybe nobody wanted to date me because I was so stressed out all the time?)

One method I used to finish college as swiftly as possible was to take the easiest classes when it came to my least favorite subjects: science and math. (Then somehow I married a scientist. But that's another story.) My easy math class was called "The Concepts of Math" and it included doing Sudoku puzzles before they were trendy. My science class of choice was called "The Plants and Animals of King College." The only animals I recall studying were birds, and we were required to learn to recognize various bird calls, none of which I remember today. My most vivid memory of the plants on our campus was learning to identify the trees on campus and becoming educated about invasive species of plants—especially certain vines that were not native to the rolling hills of Tennessee. Invasive plants grow quickly, their roots dig into the soil, and the vines begin to grow up the trunks of trees, literally taking over the growth and the beauty that God intended for that particular region.

As a class assignment, our professor took the students out into a wooded area on campus, assigning each of us a small plot of the forest. There we put our knowledge to use, pulling up invasive species of plants by their roots so that they would not destroy the natural beauty already growing there. Although I have forgotten the names of the plants and animals I studied in that class, I did learn to not let invasive plants take over.

For example, a commonly known invasive plant is English ivy. It's such a classy-looking vine, one you can imagine growing beautifully up the wall of a castle in England. In college, I worked in the fake flower department of a craft store, and we sold plenty of artificial English ivy, because people think it's beautiful! However, the actual vine grows quickly out of control, and it can dig into any cracks on the side of a building, causing damage.

Isn't that what the bitter root of offense does to us? Maybe for a moment we think it looks good on the outside, because after all, we're good at justifying why we feel offended. Yet underneath, the roots are digging into us, causing damage. It's an invasive plant, displacing something better that God intends for us.

Hebrews 12:14 says, "Make every effort to live in peace with everyone and to be holy; without holiness no one will see the Lord."

The next verse tells us to not let any bitter root grow up and cause trouble and defile us.

Some bitter roots that I must constantly pluck out include jealousy, control and offense. Jealousy tempts me to throw a temper tantrum because somebody is getting what I want. Control follows on jealousy's heels when I try to force things to go my way. That can quickly lead to anger. Or maybe I'll just stuff it all inside and not have a temper tantrum, although in my life, that looks a lot like offense. I might not yell at you, but I'm simmering inside, offended that you're not doing things the way I want. That bitter root of sin—especially the sin of offense—tears apart good sibling relationships of the sons and daughters of God. When I choose offense I'm rejecting the healing balm of forgiveness and reconciliation.

While reading about what English ivy can do to a structure, I found it interesting that it doesn't usually destroy a solid brick. Instead, the roots of the ivy dig into cracks, weakening the structure. That's exactly what the bitter roots of offense or sin will do to a Christian. You might be walking with God, living a Christian lifestyle, and your faith might even resemble a solid brick wall. Yet those cracks are places where you've been hurt before. You remember that friend who turned her back on you in high school. You have a crack in your heart from a bad breakup or a divorce in your family. A small crack, or an area of weakness that needs to be made right with God, is exactly where the enemy will try to grow the bitter root.

We must rid ourselves of the roots of bitterness that attempt to ruin us. If I allow the roots of bitterness to grow, I will become too angry to rejoice when someone else gets what I want. The roots of jealousy will choke out my ability to live with joy.

As we battle offense, let's remember that God loves reconciliation. When a friend told me that she was seeking to restore a friendship that had been broken years ago, I remember saying, "Yes! Reconciliation is so right!" I felt motivated by that conversation to seek out and reconnect with old friends with whom my relationship had been strained. Although the act of reconciliation might feel awkward, but reconciliation is undoubtedly the right decision.

If I were trying to describe God, Jesus, and the Bible in a short summary, I might say something like this: God created people, they sinned against Him, and He desperately wanted to redeem that relationship. Therefore, God sent His Son, Jesus, to pay the price and reconcile the relationship between Father God and His children. Of course, there is much more to His story, but reconciliation plays a tremendous role. God doesn't want us to be separated from Him. He also wants us to have healthy relationships with each other. There is no room for offense!

CHAPTER 13

LOOK FOR THE GOOD

Surely goodness and mercy shall follow me all the days of my life.

Psalm 23:6 (NKJV)

I'm not a natural optimist. Twenty years ago, had you eavesdropped inside my mind, you might have heard me grumbling to myself, "Well, life just sucks, but God is still good." It was so easy for me to see the difficult and unhappy side of life, even though I knew in theory that God was a good God. The battle in my mind went like this: "Wow, life sucks, but I guess God is good because He says so." Over the years I've learned that I can walk around with that pessimistic mentality, or I can try to see the good that God is doing, even in barren places.

One sunny spring morning, I set out for a run through a familiar neighborhood with paved walking trails. I passed a young woman walking her dog just as I turned left and she turned right. A few minutes later, our paths crossed again near a lake. As I ran, I saw her on the trail ahead of me, looking intently at something beside the water.

I was coming out of a forest path, uphill toward a lake. Looking up, I admired the clear blue sky, the spring green of the trees and the grass, and the way these things reflected beautifully on the still water. "Wow, God, You created such beauty!" I commented as I ran.

Then I noticed the dog walker had begun running ahead of me, and I assumed that she was also out for a run. As I neared her, she stopped running, and said something to me. I pulled out my earbuds to hear her better.

"Did you see that snake beside the path?"

"No, was there a snake?" I asked.

"Yes, that's why we were running," she responded. "I'm so scared of snakes!"

"Oh, I just thought you were running!" I commented as I began to run again.

As I began running down the trail and over the wooden footbridge, I realized that it's all a matter of perspective. Am I going to focus on the snake that's on the ground—most likely a harmless snake that obviously didn't bite me as I ran past—or am I going to focus on the beauty that God has created all around me?

Certainly, there are times when we should be aware of the snakes at our feet, but if we're only watching for snakes, we'll miss the greater beauty surrounding us. If I'm only thinking about the things in life that are unpleasant, scary, or difficult, I won't ponder the good things God is doing.

Philippians 4:8 says, "Whatever things are true, whatever things are noble, whatever things are just, whatever things are pure, whatever things are lovely, whatever things are of good report, if there is any virtue and if there is anything praiseworthy—meditate on these things." Paul writes these words just after he tells the reader to pray instead of being anxious, and God's peace will surround us.

Sometimes we simply need to lift our eyes from the path, turn our focus away from negative things, and see the good. God's goodness that is chasing us down, as David described in Psalm 23:6 (NKJV). "Surely goodness and mercy shall follow me all the days of my life." If God's goodness is following us through all of our days, let's open our eyes and acknowledge it!

Way Back in the Beginning

One January, I began reading the Bible at the beginning, and I was struck by something I read in Genesis. I kept reading the same words over and over throughout the creation account. God began the story of Creation with a barren place. In Genesis 1:1 the earth is described as being without form, empty, and dark. Then, as He filled it with abundant life, He kept saying the same words over and over again: "This is good! This is good! This is good!"

God created light, and He saw that it was good!

Then He formed the earth and sky and water, and He called it good.

After that He made plants, and He thought they were good.

Next, He created the sun and moon and stars, and He declared them to be good.

Sea creatures and birds were His next work of art, and again, He said that they are good!

Then He created animals and called them good.

Finally, God created man and woman, then gave them authority over all of His creation. He instructed them to make more humans, and He declared that the people He made were good.

When God looked at His creation, piece by piece, He declared His goodness. He called His works of art good. His creation is good! The goodness of God is woven throughout all of creation.

I should be able to take one look at the blooms on my windowsill, or the stars in a clear night sky, or my baby's cute toes, and see the goodness of God. I should even be able to see His goodness in my own toes! We don't need to look very far to see creation, and God's creation reflects His goodness.

God established a pattern as He laid the foundation of the world—He repeatedly called it good. We can see His goodness in nature, and we can also look at the work He is actively doing inside our hearts, in our lives, and in people around us. The earth is filled with the goodness of God! Surely His goodness and mercy are following us all of the days of our lives (Psalm 23).

Will I look back to see the thread that God has woven throughout my life—a thread of His faithfulness and His provision and His goodness? Even at a time when my womb and my arms were empty, or when my bank account is in need, or my circumstances might not be ideal, I can rejoice. I might feel lonely for companionship or in need of a new job, but can I still rejoice in God?

Habakkuk 3:17-18 says, "Though the fig tree does not bud and there are no grapes on the vines, though the olive crop fails and the fields produce no food, though there are no sheep in the pen and no cattle in the stalls... yet I will rejoice in the LORD, I will be joyful in God my Savior."

Will I choose joy even when I'm lacking something? Won't we always have some area of our lives that feels empty and barren, a place for God to fill? Am I determined to see His goodness right here, right now, in the land of the living?

We Can Be Both

I experienced an "ah-ha" moment when my mind was whirling with both infertility-related decisions and thoughts about a Bible study on Philippians that I was participating in. I've always struggled to appreciate the concept of contentment in the New International Version translation of Philippians 4:11 that says "I have learned to be content." I know that God's Word is right and true, however I struggle because I'm often thinking of the next thing on my agenda and not feeling content where I am in the moment. The issue at hand is that I have often felt discontent, hoping for one change or another! At that time, I was struggling to "be content" without children while still desiring to have children. That day the Holy Spirit spoke to me in a fresh way as I read this familiar passage in the New King James Version.

Philippians 4:11-12 says, "Not that I speak in regard to need, for

I have learned in whatever state I am, to be content: I know how to be abased, and I know how to abound. Everywhere and in all things I have learned both to be full and to be hungry, both to abound and to suffer need." The keyword that stood out to me is *both*.

Both. I wonder if that "secret to contentment" that Paul mentions is found in being "both." That week, in terms of my barren womb I realized that I was both empty and full. It still applies as I ponder these words years later in the middle of the unique challenges brought on in 2020 by the COVID-19 pandemic, tension throughout America, and many changes to my daily life.

I can be both: I can be totally okay, yet also not okay, because I'm trusting that God has it all figured out.

I can be both: I can be at peace while being sad. I can hope for change and be content where I am at the same time. I can desire a close friendship nearby, yet have wonderful relationships from afar.

I can be both: trusting God in difficult circumstances, and realizing that He might not answer my prayers as I desire.

I've also learned that both joy and sorrow can intermingle as we walk with God. The imagery I previously shared from Isaiah 54:1 is beautiful: "Sing, barren woman, you who never bore a child; burst into song, shout for joy, you who were never in labor; because more are the children of the desolate woman than of her who has a husband." The Lord, speaking through Isaiah, tells the barren, empty, heartbroken woman to sing with joy anyway. The word "desolate" also catches my eye in that passage. Desolate indicates lack of joy or hope, or feelings of sorrow. Somehow, we can still experience joy within sorrow.

We see grief and joy together in the Scriptures. Jesus tells his followers that "Your grief will turn to joy." (John 16:20) 2 Corinthians 6:10 says that as believers we can be "sorrowful, yet always rejoicing." In his New Testament letter to believers, James jumps right into this theme: "Consider it pure joy, my brothers and sisters, whenever you face trials of many kinds." (James 1:2) Barrenness of any type is a trial, and persevering through trials matures us, and it's possible to find joy in our sorrow.

Let's choose joy and hold onto it whenever possible. God is a God who allows us to face hard times yet surprises us with joy. He showers us with blessings in the middle of our darkness, He brings healing to our pain. God truly gives us "beauty instead of ashes." (Isaiah 61:3)

I am continually learning that I can find joy in the little things. If we look for it, we can see that God's goodness is evident even in the middle of our trials and disappointments. Sometimes finding joy in trials is simply having faith that God will give us something better later. Sometimes it's laughing at a funny incident in the middle of a stressful situation.

I am thankful to know the God who turns grief to joy, who shows me beauty in barren places. I am thankful that in my own circumstances I'm learning that God's purposes and plans for me are very good. As I trust God, I trust that my grief will turn to joy.

Living in that place of "both" is a good place to be. Maybe that's the secret to contentment: both lacking and suffering while living fully and abounding. In that place, I reach out for God, desiring to know more of His goodness. Here in the land of the living, I'm called to remember His goodness, and to faithfully persevere on the course that He has set out before me.

Take Charge of Your Thoughts

As we follow God, we need to continually think about Him. Let's read the Bible, listen to the audio Bible, read Christian books, and listen to sermons and podcasts. We should soak it up, listen to it, read it, write it down, and meditate on it. Our perspective will change for the better when we fill ourselves up with His words.

We need to speak words of life, even when feelings of disappointment are strong. It's easy, especially when we feel discouraged, to say negative things to ourselves. You might feel tempted to call yourself unkind names. You might say hurtful things. We have the potential to say all sorts of negative things in our despair.

Reading God's Word to oneself is a great starting point for speaking life. "Why are you downcast, O my soul? Why so disturbed within me? Put your hope in God, for I will yet praise Him, my Savior and my God." This verse caught my eye during my daily Bible reading on a day when I was feeling physically unwell and emotionally discouraged. I read those words in Psalm 42:5 then again in verse 11 of that same chapter. The same phrase popped up again in Psalm 43:5.

When the psalmist repeats the exact same phrases over and over again, he's trying to make a point. In these words, the writer of the Psalms is speaking life to his own soul, telling himself to not be discouraged, but to instead hope in God and to praise Him. Although he was speaking to himself, his words ministered to me also.

"Comparison is the thief of joy," is a popular phrase coined by Theodore Roosevelt. Sometimes that thief taunts me, naming the things I wish I had, such as more children or money to throw around. I might want a better house or more book sales. I can compare myself to others in so many ways.

But it does me no good to compare my situation to others. This life I live is a story God is writing. When my husband was out of work, I had to choose to be grateful for the hours of quality time we had together, the way he was able to help me with my work. I had to choose to let go of financial stress and declare that God was our provider— and that took a load off of my shoulders! I realized that my husband is not the ultimate provider, I am not the provider, our jobs are not the provider. God is our provider. Since that moment when I began to focus on God as our provider, He has provided sufficiently—and sometimes extravagantly.

I've struggled with feeling blue many years after the holidays fade and the new year begins. I've learned to choose: I could begin the cold, dark month of January curled up on the couch, on the verge of depression, legitimately grieving for the children I didn't have when we were struggling with infertility. Or I could choose to get up, take a shower, put on a little makeup, and step forth into the calling on my life. I'm called to be a wife, so I'll do my best to be a good one. I'm called to motherhood, so I'll chose to love the children in my life at any given time. I'm called to write, so here I am, wrestling through my thoughts and emotions for the world to read.

No matter our circumstances, no matter what we lack, no matter which area of life feels barren, you and I can discover the beauty of God's surprises when we choose to live out the proclamation that God is good. Even if. Even if not. Even when. Even without. Let's immerse ourselves in His Word, ask for His perspective, and look for God's goodness all around. There we'll find joy, contentment, and fulfillment, discovering beauty in barren places.

CHAPTER 14

VOLCANOES

**I lift up my eyes to the mountains—
where does my help come from?
My help comes from the Lord,
the Maker of heaven and earth.**

Psalm 121:1-2

Have you ever felt like you were about to explode? Anger and frustration are two of the more explosive emotions that I have wrestled with too often. Honestly, many exhausted evenings on the verge of such an explosion slowed me down from finishing this book. I know that the enemy of our souls doesn't want me to share these stories or to proclaim the goodness of God. The fatigue and stress and hormones that have caused these volcanic emotions in me and hindered my writing have done nothing but propel a cycle of more frustration in our family life.

Several years ago, I wrote the first draft of this book, then set it aside to follow God's prompting to publish another book about writing. Around that same time, God answered our years of prayers for a baby, and mothering a newborn shifted my writing momentum—and our entire lives—quite a bit. My husband and I adore our daughter, and at the same time, adding a baby to our lives totally rocked our world. We are happy because we had dreamed of this, but in other ways, the transition to parenthood was a difficult adjustment for our marriage.

Our daughter, the miracle baby as some might call her, was conceived after more than seven years of infertility. Although we were pursuing some medical treatments, God demonstrated His power by allowing conception to happen during a month without medical intervention. God clearly wanted to remind us that even though our fertility specialist had speculated that we only had a one percent chance of conceiving without medical assistance, God's creative power was all that we needed. Countless prayers lifted to Heaven by numerous friends, family members, and strangers resulted in a joyous announcement of our first pregnancy. Our baby girl's arrival brought much happiness and needed change, yet it jolted us out of our steady routines into this adventure called parenthood.

Having a baby offered a natural transition for me to quit my day job so that I could care for our daughter full time. Although it was my lifelong dream to be a stay-at-home-mom, it was a difficult step. We moved to a new town for my husband's new job when our baby was just a few months old. I joined a mom's group, and it was a lifesaver. There I found community with other moms of young children, and I am forever grateful. However, my husband and I were tired, older parents, my husband's job was stressful. Frequently, one or the other of us seemed to be on the verge of exploding with words, impatience, frustration, and even outbursts of resentment and anger.

Those things certainly must be dealt with, before God and with each other. But sometimes God also shakes everything up and turns circumstances around swiftly. God's divine creativity can turn a situation that has the potential to be destructive into something beautiful.

After all, as I've been learning for the past few decades, God is always making something beautiful in the barren areas of our lives.

I felt determined to finish writing this book even though I was wrestling inside: *How can I write a book about finding the goodness of God in hard places when my marriage is in a hard place right now?* I wondered. Years ago I wrote the dedication line for this book, thanking my husband for regularly pointing me toward the goodness of God. Then while trying to finish writing it, our marriage felt such pressure and stress. I asked myself, *How can I talk about God's goodness in our lives when we're dealing with this junk?*

I wanted to finish what I started, so I continued wrestling with these words and thoughts, bringing them before God.

Hawaii

One July evening, my husband told me he was considering another position at work. "Go for it," I said, even though it would require moving again. We needed some sort of change.

In August, my husband was offered that new position—in Hawaii.

We lived in Maryland at that time.

I don't want to move to Hawaii! I thought.

I prayed. We sought counsel. We discussed it. I didn't like the idea of leaving my friends in the D.C. area. I enjoyed the excitement of living near our nation's capital. Most of our family lives in North Carolina, and I wanted to live closer to them as our family grew—I didn't want to move further away! My other close friends are scattered throughout the eastern United States. I wanted to be near my people. I like familiarity.

Hawaii seemed so far away from family and friends, so unfamiliar, and everyone said that the cost of living is high there.

As I wrestled with these things, I remembered the goodness and the faithfulness of God that I had witnessed over and over in recent years. Hasn't God provided all of our needs? Didn't God provide a wonderful home for us when we moved from Virginia to Maryland? Didn't God provide a spacious place with all the natural light I had hoped for? Before that, when we moved to the D.C. suburbs for graduate school, where housing costs were very high, didn't God provide an ideal apartment that met our needs for years? Won't He provide for us in this next season? *Okay, God, I hear You. I know that You will provide all of the friendships, church community, and finances that we will need.*

I remembered that one of my favorite authors lives in Hawaii. Maybe I could be like her and become a prolific writer there. I love sunshine, and more than a decade ago I promised my husband that I would go wherever life took us, as long as we went together.

I reminded myself that God has provided for us in every step of our journey thus far. That's why I continue to "raise my Ebenezer," like in the Old Testament, writing down my experiences to remember that thus far, the Lord has helped us. He will continue to provide all that we need because He is faithful.

Hawaii. Everyone said it's beautiful there, and people call it paradise. Maybe it's what we need as a family. Maybe it's what my husband needs professionally. Maybe it's what I need as a mom and wife and writer. Maybe I'll have an opportunity in Hawaii to write the novel I've been thinking about.

As my fears and hopes mingled together in my mind, I pondered what it would look like to take the leap and accept this job so far from our comfort zone. When I shared the possibility with my friends "the Chix" via text message, one of those dear friends said, "Hey, do you remember the prayer Rebekah prayed for you back in June?" I did not remember. Thankfully, they did, and Bethany had recorded the prayers on her phone and typed them out. (I am so grateful for these friends!)

In June, we spent time in prayer at our Chix weekend. In July, my husband submitted the job application. Then August brought the job offer and our need to make a decision.

Rebekah, one of the Chix as well as a dear friend for twenty years, had prayed over my marriage back in June. She was aware of my struggles with anger and frustration. She has been my roommate, she has been my next-door neighbor, she met me when I was a teenager— she's seen me at my worst.

God showed my friend a picture of a volcano oozing lava, which she sensed would normally represent anger. But this image she saw with her mind's eye was not of a volcano that blows up and destroys, she told us. She saw a volcano oozing lava that creates a fertile land "like Hawaii."

Hawaii? Did God drop a hint about Hawaii before it was even on our radar? Did God give my friend this picture to help me make sense of my inner wrestling? Did someone use the words "fertile land" after this season of barrenness?

I wondered how I could write about finding beauty in barren places when I personally felt like a mess and a failure, so God provided a picture through my friend. He reminded me that He knows every step of the journey. He is in the details, and He can scoop us up out of a barren land and drop us right into the middle of an island bursting with life. He is the author of our faith, He's the author of our life's stories.

In this new chapter, God was moving us to Hawaii.

Rainbows

My husband accepted the job transfer, and we began preparing for the move. The process took several months, and we watched the movers haul away our household items in early January. Big snowflakes fell that day, and I declared the snowfall to be a glimpse of God's goodness, a Heavenly gift just for me as we headed to Hawaii. We visited our families, then flew to Hawaii as a family of three in mid-January. We enjoyed the sunshine and warmth when our bodies were used to dreary, gray, wintry weather. I discovered that most afternoons I could find rainbows in the sky as the sun began to set, hitting the clouds just right. Other rainbows appeared throughout the day, but I loved knowing exactly where to look in the late afternoon to see my daily rainbow.

As we adjusted to living in Hawaii, we did not know what else 2020 had in store—nobody did.

Just like every other time we moved to a new state, God provided the right home for us. Most homes are smaller in Hawaii than what we were used to on the mainland. We were glad to find an apartment that is centrally located, new and clean, with natural light, and the right price range. Along our road at that time of the year, we saw rain-filled, muddy puddles. We discovered that winter is the rainy season on Oahu.

We unpacked our home in February, and my extroverted self couldn't wait to make mom friends, visit library story time with my toddler, and connect with others in a local church. As we settled into our new routines with my husband working during the weekdays and me home with our toddler, I had hopes that she would play happily or nap well so that I could focus on my writing.

Nothing went according to plan.

We visited our library regularly for a few weeks, and were close to settling on a church to call home when a terrible virus began to wreak havoc around the world. Watching the news, we saw the effect it was having on cities such as New York, and soon communities around the world began enforcing stay-at-home mandates. Instead of getting out of the house and making friends as I had hoped, I was home most of the time with my little family.

The COVID-19 pandemic changed culture and daily life. Meanwhile, racial tension gripped America, and all of this happened as our country prepared for a presidential election. The economy struggled and hardships abounded. I felt saddened as many people that I knew were affected by death throughout this time. Death of a loved one. Death due to miscarriage, disease, old age, suicide, and murder. I know people affected by all of these.

There were so many other struggles happening around the world throughout the year. We pray for breakthrough, for a rapid end to this coronavirus, yet the world still feels like such a mess. Social media is saturated with comments about what a terrible year 2020 has been.

For me personally, even in Hawaii, life has held unusual challenges. We have experienced varying degrees of regulations and restrictions related to the pandemic, including stay-at-home-orders, closed beaches and parks, masks required, and hefty fines for those who defy the mandates. The economy that relied on tourism has struggled.

Our first year in Hawaii certainly hasn't turned out like I had imagined it would! It's been tough to connect with others when social gatherings are forbidden, covering one's face with a mask is required, and we're supposed to stay six feet away from others. As an extrovert in a new community, I struggled being home all the time. Our daughter loved it though—she loved the constant attention from her parents and thrived. I couldn't find that quiet time alone to write.

Beauty in barren places. Even the fertile land of Hawaii can feel barren during a pandemic. There can be barrenness in beautiful places too. This situation was my latest opportunity to look for God's goodness when life didn't go according to plan.

Mud Puddles

We chose to thank God through it all. We live in an air-conditioned home in this hot climate, and my husband has a stable job where he is thriving with much less stress than before. Our finances are going in the right direction. And we are so thankful for one of the greatest blessings we have received in 2020—the gift of another new life. Since I had turned 40 years old, we felt unsure about how long we would continue to try to have another baby. However, God clearly answered our prayers and I became pregnant. We are expecting a baby boy at the beginning of 2021. What a joy to have two children after many years of waiting!

In the spring, as communities began to require lockdowns, the island of Oahu enforced their first COVID-19 stay-at-home order. I didn't like the sound of that. I was new here, ready to get out and make friends and explore Hawaii! I didn't want to stay home all of the time. Ugh!

I looked out the window late in the afternoon when order was announced, and I could see a marvelous rainbow. That particular rainbow reminded me that we have an all-knowing Creator with a Heavenly perspective who loves us deeply. He saw all of this coming:

the pandemic, racial issues, political disagreements, wildfires, hurricanes, economic trouble, political tension. You name it, God knew it already. He was not taken aback when all of these dynamics collided and hit our country hard within one year.

That same evening, just before the first lockdown took effect, our little family decided to go for a drive and watch the sunset over the North Shore. As we walked down the driveway toward our car, I noticed that the rainbow continued to linger overhead. It hung out in the sky for a couple of hours that evening. As I passed by one of those springtime puddles along our road, I saw a reflection of the rainbow in the muddy water.

I paused to take a picture, and I continued to think about that puddle throughout the year. Am I going to focus on the messy, yucky, muddy puddle that 2020 resembles? Or will I look for the rainbow in the middle of the mess?

It might be particularly easy right now to look at our circumstances and situations and declare how bad they are. However, if we slow down and look around, we can always find God's goodness, because He is always good, even in the middle of a mud puddle or a pandemic. Once again, I remind myself that "the earth is full of the goodness of the Lord." (Psalm 33:5 NKJV) If this earth is full of God's goodness, we can look for it and find it. As we persevere in opening our eyes to His goodness, we mature and grow in faith.

This year has changed me and it has changed how our family does life. It has improved our marriage. It has slowed me down, refocused me, and provided a new normal. I haven't enjoyed all of the changes, but I am trusting that this divine redirecting and reshaping is ultimately being worked out for God's glory and for my good.

He's Writing Our Stories

Our God, who writes the script differently than I would have imagined, knows what He's doing. He knows the best storyline for your life as well. I don't understand why it took so long, but I'm thankful that He has given us two children after years of barrenness. God was with us when my husband and I took long walks on the Carolina coast over the years. Then He opened up the door for a job transfer, taking us to a distant seashore. God brought us to a place where we can grow and reconnect with each other, to a place where we can be refreshed as a family.

Maybe you're reading this and wishing that God would dramatically open up a door of change for you right now. Sometimes He does that suddenly.

Other times, we wait in the barren place and persevere through the valleys. No matter where you are, seek Him, and look for His goodness in the barren places. When your life feels empty, in the places where you are lacking, whether in relationships, finances, emotions, or anything else, you can find His goodness, His love, and His provision. I expect that your circumstances will eventually change, but if not? He's still good.

Sometimes life is just hard. Our jobs and workplaces are often difficult to face day after day, but work is necessary so we can afford our homes, our food, and other necessities. Relationships can be difficult, even when we're determined to persevere. The hard stuff you're facing might be infertility, a physical barrenness. Maybe you're grieving a loss, a death or a divorce. Maybe you're grieving because something you hoped for didn't happen. In the ebb and the flow of life, in fullness and barrenness, God constantly demonstrates that He's good and faithful.

Even when our emotions make us feel like we're going to explode, God is able to change circumstances and He is able to change us. God's beauty and His goodness can be found in every barren place when we look for them with new eyes and a fresh perspective. He might do something drastic, like pick us up from a Maryland winter and transplant us to the Hawaii sunshine. He might immerse you in a similar place of physical beauty. Or He might leave you in a cold northern climate, but show you glimpses of His goodness through wildflowers and ice storms. He might show you His creativity in the desert. He might allow hardships in your life without shifting your circumstances, but through it He will draw you close to Himself and show you His goodness. He might say that it's time for something new and fresh, then totally rock your world and your circumstances. He might not. Yet He's always good.

Maybe you're just stumbling into the goodness of God, growing in awareness that He is good toward you even though your current circumstances are tough. Ask Him to increase your desire for His beauty. Ask God to show you more of His goodness. Reach for it. He is doing remarkable things in your life, so pause to look for small miracles and write them down. Surely His goodness will follow us all of the days of our lives and we can dwell in His presence forever. Look at the story He's writing with your life and choose to taste and see His goodness.

Word-of-mouth is crucial for any author to succeed. If you enjoyed this book, please tell your friends and leave a review on Amazon. Even a sentence or two makes a difference and is much appreciated! I invite you to follow me on social media and subscribe to my newsletter. You can find me through my website: www.hopeduringinfertility.com. Thank you

NOTES

Chapter 7: Lost and Found

1) Robert Robinson, "Come Thou Fount of Every Blessing" public domain

Chapter 8: Fog

1) John Piper, Twitter @JohnPiper, March 1, 2016, https://twitter.com/johnpiper/status/704653441533132800

Chapter 11: Offended by God

1) Kelly Streiff, Instagram @kelly.streiff, November 18, 2019, https://www.instagram.com/p/B5BPhNqHjwL/

Weblinks active at the time of publication.

ACKNOWLEDGEMENTS

Thank you to my husband, Mike. I love the way you focus on God's goodness. Thank you for helping me find the time I needed to finish this project!

Thank you to Lydia Herman and Kimberly Menken for your invaluable edits of the full manuscript. Thank you for encouraging me to persevere!

Thank you to each person who read either a very rough draft or a nearly-finished piece of this manuscript. Your comments and feedback have been vital. I could not write and publish without the support of friends, family, and social media contacts.

Thank you to Jennifer Cabezon for allowing me to share stories about our shared adventures in Panama.

Thank you to Kelly Streiff for allowing me to share your insights from Daniel 3.

Thank you to the Chix for allowing me to write about you, but most of all, thank you for decades of friendship and speaking into my life.

Thank you to other friends and family members for allowing me to write about our shared experiences.

Thanks to my social media community for chiming in when I asked questions related to this book. Thank you for reading my words!

Thank you to Natasha Metzler for writing the foreword and encouraging me along the way.

Thank you to Rebekah Hauck for designing yet another beautiful book cover.

ABOUT THE AUTHOR

Betsy Herman currently writes from Hawaii, where she recharges by reading a good book or getting outside to explore the beaches and soak up the sun. She and her husband are grateful to have become parents later in life, and you'll most often find her at home, fueling with coffee to keep up with her little ones. She is passionate about writing her way through life's challenges, and she wants to encourage you put your hope in God regardless of what you're going through.

When Infertility Books Are Not Enough: Embracing Hope During Infertility

Does your desire for motherhood seem impossible? Have your hopes led to disappointment? Are you facing delayed dreams? What do you do with an empty womb and a broken heart? You've dreamed of being a mother ever since you were a young girl, but these dreams remain just that. Maybe you face secondary infertility, and your child does not yet know the joy of growing up with siblings. Or, perhaps you would like to gain some insight about this struggle to conceive, to help someone that you care about.

This is Betsy's story of the emotional roller coaster called infertility. Despite her pain and disappointment, she began to realize that God is for her and not against her. Throughout her challenging personal journey, Betsy shares her steadfast understanding that God is good, regardless of the circumstances. If you need encouragement in your delayed dreams, then this book is for you. You are not alone!

Seasons: A Picture Book

Children and adults alike will enjoy experiencing the four seasons from a child's perspective. While traversing spring, summer, autumn, and winter, readers are reminded of God's unchanging goodness regardless of what each season brings. These timeless, classic illustrations and rhyming lyrics will delight readers of all ages as it teaches children about the four seasons. Illustrated by Karen Schneider.

OTHER BOOKS BY BETSY HERMAN
(available on Amazon and through other online retailers)

Write Your Story: Straightforward Steps for (Finally) Writing and Publishing Your Book

Do you want to write a book but don't know where to begin? Do you worry about how to find a publisher? Maybe you've begun writing but need encouragement to finish. *Write Your Story* is the blueprint you're looking for.

Learn how to:
- find the time to write
- overcome writer's block
- battle the fear of publishing
- understand the editorial process
- consider self-publishing options
- engage with your audience
- estimate the cost
- launch and market your book

Packed with practical information that's especially pertinent to Christian authors, *Write Your Story* guides you from the initial idea to the finished product.

Printed in Great Britain
by Amazon